THE
SIZZLING
SAUSAGE
COOKBOOK

STORY FARM

WINTER PARK • MIAMI
SANTA BARBARA

FAMILY OWNED SINCE 1945

Johnsonville®

THE
SIZZLING
SAUSAGE
COOKBOOK

MEGAN NEHLS WITH SHELLY STAYER

Published in the United States of America by Story Farm, LLC.
Printed in China by Crash Paper of Playa del Rey, CA.

Library of Congress Cataloging-in-Publication data
is available upon request.
ISBN: 978-0-9966038-8-1

EDITORIAL DIRECTOR Ashley Fraxedas
ART DIRECTOR Jason Farmand
PRODUCTION MANAGER Tina Dahl
EDITORIAL ASSISTANTS Marcela Oliveira, Caitlin McCarthy
COPY EDITORS Karen Cakebread, Cassandra Palmer
INDEXING Amy Hall
RECIPE DEVELOPMENT Julia Griffiths & The Kitchen
                             at Johnsonville

Second Edition: February 2018
10 9 8 7 6 5 4 3 2

CONTENTS

WELCOME TO THE

JOHNSONVILLE® SIZZLING SAUSAGE GRILL™
COOKBOOK!

––––––––––

ON THE PAGES that follow, you'll find dozens of easy recipes that will help you enjoy your Johnsonville® Sizzling Sausage Grill™ to the fullest and make you the star of any occasion, whether it's a quick family dinner, a game day party, a festive gathering with friends or snack time for the kids.

But first, I have a little confession to make: When it comes to cooking on an outdoor grill, well, I'm not very good at it.

There, I've said it.

I come from a big family of expert grillers, some of whom have made grilling an art form. But not me. Whenever I try it, everything that can go wrong does go wrong. The fire's too hot; the fire's not hot enough; there's too much smoke; the meat's overcooked; the meat's undercooked. On and on and on.

That's why I invented the Johnsonville® Sizzling Sausage Grill™. I wanted to make grilling sausage easy. I wanted to enjoy "guess-less grilling."

EVEN THE MOST accomplished grillers will admit that grilling the perfect sausage in the traditional manner is not quite as easy as it might look. You have to stand right by the grill and keep an eye on everything, constantly turning the sausage and making sure there isn't a flare-up from down below. Even then, you can't be sure whether the sausage is done. And if you slice it to check—oops—there go all those succulent juices. Nothing worse than a dried-out sausage.

After much trial and error—five years to be exact—I finally perfected the grill and its patented sensor probe. It's the little doohickey that pokes out from the top cooking surface. And it makes sure that each and every sausage is cooked to a consistent and ideal temperature—160 degrees Fahrenheit.

There's no preheating and no need to add oil to the cooking surface. All you have to do is place the sausage in the slots (you can cook five at a time, or just one), close the top, go about your business and—voila!—15 minutes later, you'll hear the ding that means your sausage is done!

OF COURSE, now that grilling sausage is easier than ever before—and more fun!—you'll need lots of ideas for sharing all this sausage goodness with your family and friends. We've spent years perfecting our recipes at Johnsonville® Sausage. We've tested the ones you'll find here based on their easy adaptability to the Johnsonville® Sizzling Sausage Grill™. We hope you'll enjoy them as much as we do.

––––––––––

YOURS IN GUESS-LESS GRILLING,

Shelly Stayer

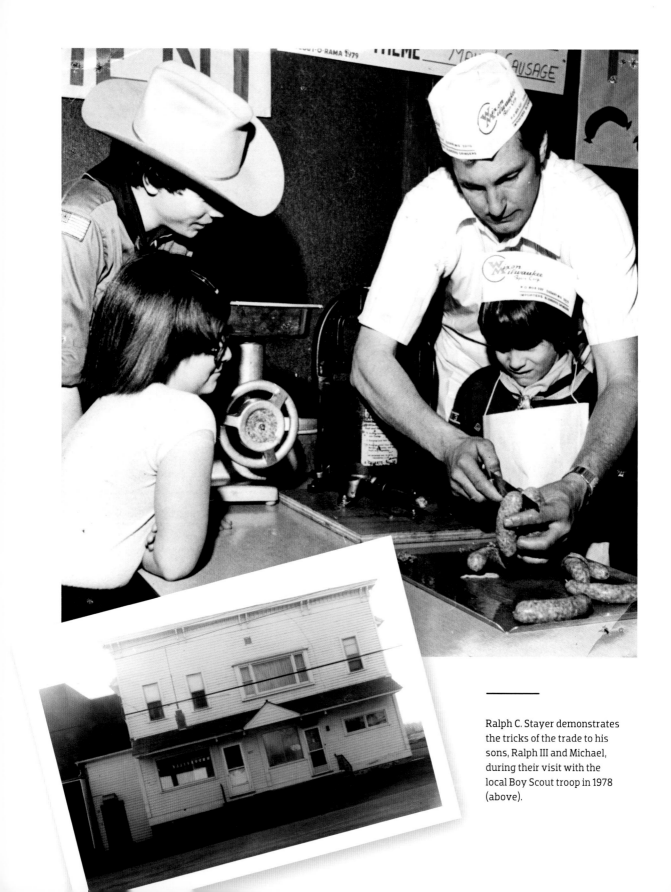

Ralph C. Stayer demonstrates the tricks of the trade to his sons, Ralph III and Michael, during their visit with the local Boy Scout troop in 1978 (above).

FROM THE BEGINNING

IT WAS 1945 when Ralph F. Stayer and his wife, Alice, moved from Milwaukee to the German farming country of eastern Wisconsin. Seeking their version of the American Dream, the Stayers bought a small meat market in the hamlet of Johnsonville, where the population at the time was just 65.

Not long after their arrival, having attended several local fundraisers where hamburgers and bratwursts were grilled and sold, Ralph noticed two things: Hamburgers outsold bratwurst five to one. And many of bratwursts were tossed uneaten into trash containers.

So, Ralph decided to make a great-tasting brat that would turn the tables. He used a secret recipe that dated back to 19th-century Austria, one that had been handed down through the Stayer family. Ralph's sausages were an immediate hit. Within a year his brats were outselling hamburgers five to one at charitable events.

Such were the humble beginnings of Johnsonville.

In the 1950s, business was booming. To keep up with the growing demand for Johnsonville Sausage, Alice Stayer (second from left) recruited local women to assist in sales.

The growing Johnsonville staff pictured in 1964, including Alice Stayer (third from right).

By the 1950s, demand for Johnsonville led the Stayers to open retail markets in three neighboring communities. When their son, Ralph C. Stayer, graduated from the University of Notre Dame in 1965, he joined the family business and began expanding it, first regionally and then nationally. By the late 1990s, Johnsonville Sausage was available in most major supermarkets and in all 50 states.

Over the years, Johnsonville, while never straying far from its roots, has proven itself a leader and innovator in its field. It is committed to animal well-being and is constantly improving its equipment and facilities, educating its employees in ethical treatment practices and actively pursuing new technology to further enhance its handling practices.

The company is also committed to sustainability, meaning it works in a way that shows people it cares about its employees, customers and the planet as much as it cares about its business— always with an eye on the future.

Johnsonville, now based in Sheboygan, Wisconsin, remains privately owned with some 1,600 employee-members, each of whom takes ownership in the company products. Johnsonville is proud to now be the leading sausage manufacturer in the United States, with products sold worldwide in 40 countries and counting.

1

STARTERS

SERVINGS **24** | PREP **25** MIN | COOK **8** MIN

COOK TIME
(30)
MIN OR LESS

SPICY SAUSAGE
QUESO

Tired of the same old chips and dip? This cheese-luscious version will score big points and be the MVP of your snack table.

INGREDIENTS

- 1 (19-ounce) package Johnsonville® Hot Italian Sausage Links
- 2 pounds Velveeta® cheese, cubed
- 1 (16-ounce) jar chunky salsa
- 1 tablespoon fennel seeds, crushed
- 2 teaspoons garlic powder
- 1 teaspoon anise seeds, crushed
- ¼ teaspoon dried basil
- Garlic toast

1 Grill sausages on the Johnsonville® Sizzling Sausage Grill™ (or cook using your favorite method). Cool slightly; dice and set aside.

2 Meanwhile, place cheese in a large microwave-safe bowl.

3 Microwave on high for 6 minutes or until melted, stirring every 2 minutes.

4 Stir in the salsa, seasonings and sausage.

5 Microwave for 2 more minutes or until heated through.

6 Serve with garlic toast.

SAUSAGE
DEVILED EGGS

The texture and spice of the sausage pairs well with the creaminess of the egg yolk filling. Perfect to take to a party or summer barbecue.

1   Grill sausages on the Johnsonville® Sizzling Sausage Grill™ (or cook using your favorite method). Cool slightly; dice and set aside.

2   Meanwhile, slice eggs in half lengthwise. Remove yolks and grate on the small holes of a box grater into a mixing bowl. Add mustard, mayonnaise, hot sauce, salt and pepper, and mix thoroughly. Place yolk mixture in a large, sealable plastic bag.

3   Fill egg whites halfway with sausage. Cut off a corner of the plastic bag, and pipe yolk mixture into egg whites over sausage, overfilling the whites. Top yolk mixture with more sausage.

4   Refrigerate until ready to serve.

INGREDIENTS

- 2 links Johnsonville® Mild or Hot Italian Sausage

- 1 dozen eggs, hard-boiled

- 1-2 teaspoons Dijon mustard

- ⅓ cup high-quality mayonnaise

- A few dashes of your favorite hot sauce

- ½ teaspoon kosher salt

- A few turns of freshly ground black pepper

CHEESY PEPPER POPPERS

COOK TIME
30
MIN OR LESS

When brats meet jalapeños, it's a marriage made in spicy heaven. Just what you need to turn up the heat at your next get-together.

1 Grill brats on the Johnsonville® Sizzling Sausage Grill™ (or cook using your favorite method). Cool slightly, then dice finely.

2 Preheat oven to 400°F.

3 In a small bowl, combine sausage, cream cheese and Parmesan.

4 Spoon mixture into prepared peppers.

5 Arrange filled peppers on an ungreased baking sheet. Bake for 12 to 15 minutes or until lightly browned.

SERVING SUGGESTION: Serve poppers with your favorite ranch or blue cheese dressing.

INGREDIENTS

1 (19-ounce) package Johnsonville® Original Brats

1 (8-ounce) package cream cheese, softened

1⅓ cups Parmesan cheese, shredded

20 large jalapeño peppers, cut in half lengthwise, seeds removed

★ SAFETY TIP ★

Wear disposable gloves when cutting hot peppers; the oils can burn your skin. Avoid touching your face.

ORIGINAL BRAT
QUESADILLAS

COOK TIME
30
MIN OR LESS

Pickles and mustard share tortilla real estate with cheese and Johnsonville® Original Bratwurst. The result is a marvelous mixture of textures and tastes.

1   (19-ounce) package Johnsonville® Original Brats

10   large flour tortillas

5   tablespoons German-style mustard

20   slices Muenster cheese

1   cup dill pickle slices

1   medium yellow onion, chopped

1   Grill brats on the Johnsonville® Sizzling Sausage Grill™ (or cook using your favorite method). Cool slightly; cut into ¼-inch slices and set aside.

2   Spread 5 tortillas with mustard.

3   Top each tortilla with 2 cheese slices; divide sausage slices, pickle slices and chopped onion evenly among tortillas.

4   Top each tortilla with an additional 2 slices of cheese and cover with another tortilla.

5   Press down slightly on top of tortillas to marry ingredients together.

6   Heat over medium heat on an indoor grill pan or in the oven until heated through.

7   Slice into wedges and serve immediately.

COOK TIME
30
MIN OR LESS

INGREDIENTS

- 1 (19-ounce) package Johnsonville® Original Brats
- 1 tablespoon olive oil
- 1½ tablespoons garlic, minced
- 1 cup onion, thinly sliced
- 1 cup carrots, shredded
- 4 cups cabbage, shredded
- ¼ cup soy sauce
- ¼ teaspoon white pepper
- 40-45 potsticker wrappers*
- 2 tablespoons vegetable oil
- 2 tablespoons water, plus more for brushing

  Dipping sauce

  * Wonton wrappers may be substituted for potsticker wrappers.

BRATWURST POTSTICKERS

The fusion of heavy-hitting brats with the finesse of Asian seasonings shows that the flavors of Johnsonville® are truly universal.

1 Grill brats on the Johnsonville® Sizzling Sausage Grill™ (or cook using your favorite method). Cool slightly; dice and set aside.

2 Meanwhile, heat olive oil in a large skillet. Add garlic, onion, carrots and cabbage, and sauté until tender.

3 Add soy sauce, white pepper and sausage; stir to combine. Remove skillet from heat.

4 Spoon 1 tablespoon of meat filling onto each potsticker wrapper.

5 Brush the edge of each wrapper with water, then fold in half and seal.

6 In a clean skillet, heat vegetable oil and brown potstickers on both sides.

7 Add 2 tablespoons water to skillet, cover and allow to steam for 5 to 7 minutes. Serve with dipping sauce.

SAUSAGE
BRUSCHETTA

COOK TIME
30
MIN OR LESS

Be transported to the Italian countryside with this traditional dish. It's great by itself, but what makes this dish truly memorable is mild Italian sausage slices. The seasonings of the sausage bring the flavors together for a delicious appetizer.

1 Grill sausages on the Johnsonville® Sizzling Sausage Grill™ (or cook using your favorite method). Let cool slightly; cut into quarters lengthwise, then into slices.

2 Preheat oven to 450°F.

3 While sausage is cooking, whisk together 3 tablespoons olive oil, basil, balsamic vinegar, garlic, salt and pepper. Stir in tomatoes and set aside.

4 Brush one side of each bread slice with olive oil and place oil-side down on a baking sheet. Bake for 5 minutes or until golden brown.

5 Remove bread from oven and turn over. Top with sausage, tomato mixture and Parmesan cheese.

6 Bake for 2 to 3 more minutes or until cheese melts. Serve immediately.

INGREDIENTS

1 (19-ounce) package Johnsonville® Mild Italian Sausage Links

3 tablespoons olive oil, plus more for brushing

2 tablespoons fresh basil, chopped

2 teaspoons balsamic vinegar

1 clove garlic, minced

½ teaspoon salt

¼ teaspoon pepper

2 cups tomatoes, chopped

10 slices French baguette or Italian bread (½ inch thick)

½ cup Parmesan cheese, shredded

SERVINGS 10   ⏱ **PREP 20 MIN**   ⏱ **COOK 25 MIN**

1 (19-ounce) package Johnsonville® Hot 'n Spicy Brats

¼ cup red bell pepper, diced

¼ cup yellow bell pepper, diced

¼ cup green bell pepper, diced

¼ cup red onion, diced

1 (10-ounce) can diced tomatoes with green chilies, drained

1 tablespoon fresh cilantro, coarsely chopped

Zest and juice of ½ lime

1¼ cups Monterey Jack cheese, shredded

20 (6-inch) flour tortillas

HOT & SPICY
TAQUITOS

COOK TIME
30
MIN OR LESS

This simple and flavorful Mexican-inspired dish is muy simpatico when served with guacamole, sliced black olives, salsa and a side of sour cream flavored with cumin or chipotle seasoning.

———

1   Grill brats on the Johnsonville® Sizzling Sausage Grill™ (or cook using your favorite method). Cool slightly and dice.

2   Preheat oven to 350°F.

3   Place brats in a large bowl; add peppers, onion, tomatoes with green chilies, cilantro, lime zest and juice, and cheese. Mix well to combine.

4   Place 2 heaping teaspoons of the mixture on one edge of each tortilla. Roll up jellyroll-style. Place stuffed taquitos, seam side down, on a baking sheet to keep them from unrolling.

5   Bake for 8 to 10 minutes, then serve.

SERVINGS 2 | PREP 10 MIN | COOK 15 MIN

AVOCADO TOAST
WITH CHORIZO & EGGS

COOK TIME 30 MIN OR LESS

INGREDIENTS

- 2 links Johnsonville® Chorizo Sausage
- 4 slices sourdough or your favorite bread
- Olive oil
- 2 avocados
- 4 eggs
- Salt and pepper, to taste

Whether starting your day or kicking off an evening's entertaining, this zinger gets things going in a big way.

1. Grill sausages on the Johnsonville® Sizzling Sausage Grill™ (or cook using your favorite method). Cool slightly; cut into ½-inch slices and set aside.
2. While sausage is cooking, toast bread, slice avocados and cook eggs to your liking.
3. Drizzle each piece of toasted bread with olive oil; top with avocado, chorizo and an egg. Sprinkle with salt and pepper.

ANTIPASTI
SKEWER

COOK TIME
30
MIN OR LESS

These skewers are both packed with flavor and easy to serve at your next dinner party. They really start the meal out on the right foot.

1   Grill Italian sausage on the Johnsonville® Sizzling Sausage Grill™ (or cook using your favorite method). Cool slightly; cut into 1-inch pieces and set aside.

2   Thread 1 small or ½ large basil leaf onto a skewer. Add a piece of roasted red pepper, artichoke and sausage, arranging them so that skewer can stand up on sausage end. Repeat with remaining ingredients to make about two dozen skewers.

2

SALADS
— AND —
SIDES

SERVINGS **4–6** | ⏱ PREP **10** MIN | ⏱ COOK **15** MIN

- 1 (19-ounce) package Johnsonville® Mild or Hot Italian Sausage Links
- ¼ cup olive oil
- 2 tablespoons red wine vinegar
- 1 jar artichoke hearts, drained and quartered
- 1 clove garlic, minced
- 2 bunches kale
- ⅓ cup red onion, diced small
- 1 cup cherry tomatoes, halved
- Parmesan cheese
- Salt and pepper, to taste

KALE & ITALIAN SAUSAGE
SALAD

COOK TIME **30** MIN OR LESS

You can use any kind of kale for this salad. Try the curly varieties if you want a little extra crunch.

1 Grill sausages on the Johnsonville® Sizzling Sausage Grill™ (or cook using your favorite method). Cool slightly; cut into ½-inch slices and set aside.

2 Meanwhile, whisk together olive oil and red wine vinegar.

3 In a large bowl, combine all remaining ingredients except cheese, salt and pepper. Add oil-and-vinegar mixture and toss to combine. Sprinkle with cheese, then season with salt and pepper.

ITALIAN
CHOPPED SALAD

COOK TIME
30
MIN OR LESS

The secret to a perfect chopped salad is making sure the main ingredients are as close to a uniform size as possible. And don't just drizzle the dressing. Make sure you toss the salad so that every piece gets a coating.

1 Grill sausages on the Johnsonville® Sizzling Sausage Grill™ (or cook using your favorite method). Cool slightly; cut into ½-inch slices and set aside.

2 Meanwhile, whisk together olive oil, red wine vinegar and mustard.

3 In a large bowl, combine sausage with all remaining ingredients except salt and pepper. Add mustard mixture and toss to combine. Season with salt and pepper.

INGREDIENTS

1 (19-ounce) package Johnsonville® Mild or Hot Italian Sausage Links

½ cup olive oil

½ cup red wine vinegar

1 tablespoon Dijon mustard

3 cups romaine hearts, chopped

1 jar artichoke hearts, drained and diced small

1 can chickpeas, drained and rinsed

¾ cup cucumber, diced small

2 cloves garlic, minced

1 cup grape tomatoes, halved

2 pepperoncini peppers, diced small

1 cup provolone cheese, diced small

Salt and pepper, to taste

ANTIPASTI SALAD

COOK TIME
30
MIN OR LESS

Looking for a dish to bring the occasion together? Few can top an approachable antipasti platter with a little something for everyone.

1   Grill sausages on the Johnsonville® Sizzling Sausage Grill™ (or cook using your favorite method). Cool slightly; cut into ½-inch slices and set aside.

2   Spread lettuce on a large serving platter.

3   Top with olives, cheese, peppers, artichoke hearts, tomatoes and sausage.

4   To serve, drizzle with dressing.

┤ INGREDIENTS ├

1 (19-ounce) package Johnsonville® Mild or Hot Italian Sausage Links

1 head romaine lettuce, cored and cut into 3-inch pieces

½ cup black olives

½ cup Greek olives

½ cup fresh mozzarella, diced medium

½ cup sweet red peppers, diced medium

½ cup artichoke hearts, drained and quartered

½ cup grape tomatoes

1 cup Italian dressing

INGREDIENTS

- 1 (19-ounce) package Johnsonville® Sweet Italian Sausage Links
- 2 packages prewashed spring mix
- 1 quart fresh strawberries, quartered
- 2 Granny Smith apples, diced medium
- ½ cup walnuts
- ½ cup feta cheese, diced small
- 4 tablespoons apple cider vinegar
- 4 tablespoons honey
- 2 tablespoons canola oil

STRAWBERRY & APPLE
SWEET ITALIAN SAUSAGE SALAD

COOK TIME
30
MIN OR LESS

Apples and sausage were made for each other. And they're made even better with the fresh surprise of strawberries.

————

1 Grill sausages on the Johnsonville® Sizzling Sausage Grill™ (or cook using your favorite method). Cool slightly; cut into ½-inch slices and set aside.

2 In a large bowl, combine spring mix, strawberries, apples, walnuts, cheese and sausage.

3 In a small bowl, combine vinegar, honey and oil. Pour over salad mixture; toss and serve.

INGREDIENTS

- 1 (19-ounce) package Johnsonville® Mild or Hot Italian Sausage Links
- 1 pound tri-colored rotini pasta
- 1 cup broccoli florets
- 1½ cups English cucumber, thickly sliced
- 1 red bell pepper, diced medium
- 1 can black olives, drained
- ½ red onion, diced small
- 1½ cups Italian dressing

CLASSIC ITALIAN
PASTA SALAD

COOK TIME
30
MIN OR LESS

There are countless variations on the theme of pasta salad. This is our go-to version, which usually disappears fast.

1 Grill sausages on the Johnsonville® Sizzling Sausage Grill™ (or cook using your favorite method). Cool slightly; cut into ½-inch slices and set aside.

2 Meanwhile, bring a large pot of water to a boil and add pasta; cook until al dente. Add broccoli and cook for 2 more minutes. Drain and set aside.

3 In a large bowl, combine cucumber, pepper, olives, onion and sausage. Add pasta and broccoli, and stir to combine. Top with dressing, and toss to coat.

4 Store in an airtight container in the refrigerator. (For best results, store for 4 hours in advance of enjoying.) Toss and serve.

COOK TIME
30
MIN OR LESS

ITALIAN SAUSAGE
WITH ROSEMARY & MUSHROOM STUFFING

A great twist on an old favorite, this adds just the right kick to that same old stuffing recipe.

---

1   Preheat oven to 350°F.

2   Grill sausages on the Johnsonville® Sizzling Sausage Grill™ (or cook using your favorite method).

3   While the sausage is cooking, combine breadcrumbs, cheese, rosemary, parsley, bacon bits and egg.

4   In a medium skillet, sauté green pepper, onion and mushrooms for 1 to 2 minutes. Add to breadcrumb mixture, and stir to combine.

5   Once links are cool enough to handle, split lengthwise, being careful not to cut all the way through and leaving the ends intact. Place in a baking pan.

6   Spoon equal amounts of stuffing into split sausages.

7   Bake for 8 to 10 minutes, or until the internal temperature reaches 165°F.

INGREDIENTS

- 1 (19-ounce) package Johnsonville® Mild Italian Sausage Links
- ½ cup panko breadcrumbs
- ½ cup shredded Parmesan cheese
- 1 teaspoon fresh rosemary, minced
- 1 tablespoon fresh parsley, minced
- 1 tablespoon real bacon bits
- 1 egg, beaten
- ¼ cup green pepper, finely chopped
- ¼ cup onion, finely chopped
- ¼ cup mushrooms, finely chopped

- 1 link Johnsonville® Four Cheese Italian Sausage
- 2 tablespoons vegetable oil
- ½ medium onion, diced
- 1 pouch Uncle Ben's® Ready Rice® Butter & Garlic Flavored
- 2 cloves garlic, minced
- ½ (6-ounce) bag baby spinach
- ½ cup shredded Parmesan cheese, divided

FOUR CHEESE SAUSAGE & RICE
FLORENTINE

COOK TIME **30** MIN OR LESS

For quick and easy Italian goodness, this is ideal when you don't have much time to spare. And using Uncle Ben's Ready Rice will take minutes off your prep time.

1   Grill sausage on the Johnsonville® Sizzling Sausage Grill™ (or cook using your favorite method). Cool slightly; cut into ½-inch slices and set aside.

2   While the sausage is cooking, heat oil in a large sauté pan. Add onion and sauté until soft and transparent.

3   While onion cooks, heat Uncle Ben's® Ready Rice® in the microwave according to package instructions.

4   Add garlic and sausage to pan with onion.

5   Add rice and spinach. Cook until mixture is well combined and spinach has wilted.

6   Add half of the cheese; mix until melted.

7   Top with remaining cheese and serve.

SAUSAGE & VEGETABLE
RISOTTO

Too often risotto is a dish we enjoy only when dining out. This easy rendition brings the taste of a fine restaurant to the comfort of your home.

1　Grill sausages on the Johnsonville® Sizzling Sausage Grill™ (or cook using your favorite method). Cool slightly; cut into ½-inch slices and set aside.

2　Meanwhile, pour chicken stock into a saucepan. (If using fresh herbs, add them to stock.) Bring stock to a gentle simmer; cover until ready to use.

3　In a large saucepan, heat extra-light olive oil over medium heat; add onion and sauté until tender and translucent, about 5 minutes.

4　Add mushrooms and cook, stirring until mushrooms are just wilted, about 2 minutes.

5　Mix in rice and cook, stirring until kernels are hot and coated with oil, about 2 more minutes.

6　Add wine and stir continuously until liquid is absorbed.

7　Using a ladle, add hot stock about ½ cup at a time, stirring constantly and making sure stock has been absorbed before adding more to rice. Continue adding ½ cup of stock, stirring rice constantly and gently.

8　When rice is about half-cooked, or only 1½ cups of stock remain, add asparagus pieces and continue stirring.

INGREDIENTS

- 1　(19-ounce) package Johnsonville® Mild Italian Sausage Links
- 5¼　cups chicken stock
- 3　sprigs fresh basil, oregano or thyme (optional)
- 4　tablespoons extra-light olive oil
- 1　medium yellow onion, finely chopped
- 2　cups white button mushrooms, wiped clean and sliced about ¼ inch thick
- 2　cups arborio rice or medium-grain risotto rice
- ½　cup dry white wine
- ½　pound asparagus, stemmed and cut into 1-inch pieces
- ½　cup peas, fresh shelled or frozen
- 　　Salt and pepper, to taste
- ⅓　cup shredded Parmesan cheese, for garnish
- 2　tablespoons extra-virgin olive oil
- 　　Grated Parmesan cheese, for garnish

9 When 1 cup of liquid remains in pan, stir in sausage and peas, and season with salt and pepper. Continue stirring. Risotto is done when rice grains are creamy on the outside and firm yet tender to the bite, about 20 to 25 minutes total.

10 When risotto is just right, remove from heat and stir in shredded cheese.

11 Spoon into large soup bowls and top with grated cheese. For the finishing touch, drizzle with extra-virgin olive oil. Serve immediately.

NOTE: Rice varies, so you may not need all of the stock, or you may need more. If more liquid is required, you can add simmering water in place of the extra broth. You should taste for doneness along the way.

TWICE-BAKED ITALIAN
SWEET POTATO

Break up with old-school twice-baked potatoes and start going out with these sweeties. Load on the toppings and fall quickly in love.

1. Preheat oven to 375°F.

2. Line a baking sheet with foil. Use a fork to poke potatoes once or twice on both sides. Arrange potatoes on prepared baking sheet and bake until fork-tender, about 40 to 60 minutes.

3. While potatoes are baking, grill Italian sausages on the Johnsonville® Sizzling Sausage Grill™ (or cook using your favorite method). Cool slightly; dice and set aside.

4. Meanwhile, heat olive oil in a large skillet, then add leeks, sage, thyme, salt and pepper. When ingredients start to sizzle, lower heat and continue cooking, stirring frequently, until leeks are soft and edges start to turn golden, 10 to 15 minutes. Add leeks and herbs to sausage, and cover to keep warm.

5. Once potatoes are baked, allow to cool slightly and cut in half lengthwise. Carefully scoop out flesh into a large bowl, keeping skin intact by leaving ⅛ to ¼ inch of flesh in potato shells. Arrange empty potato skins on the same baking sheet until ready to fill.

6. Mash scooped flesh with a potato masher until smooth. Stir in sour cream. Fold sausage and leeks into mashed potato mixture, then mix in ½ cup of cheese. Mound filling into potato skins, and sprinkle with remaining ¼ cup of cheese.

7. Preheat broiler. Broil stuffed potatoes on middle rack of oven until cheese bubbles and starts to turn golden-brown, about 4 minutes.

8. Garnish with a sprinkle of green onion and serve immediately.

INGREDIENTS

- 5 small sweet potatoes (about 8 ounces each)
- 1 (19-ounce) package Johnsonville® Sweet Italian Sausage Links
- 2 tablespoons olive oil
- ¾ pound leeks, white and light-green parts only, quartered lengthwise and thinly sliced (about 1½ cups)
- 1 teaspoon fresh sage, chopped, or ½ teaspoon, dried
- ¼ teaspoon thyme
- ¼ teaspoon salt
- ¼ teaspoon black pepper
- ⅔ cup sour cream
- ¾ cup grated Gruyère cheese, divided
- ¼ cup green onions, thinly sliced, for garnish

SAUSAGE & ROOT VEGETABLE
HASH

COOK TIME
30
MIN OR LESS

It's earthy, it's easy and it's guaranteed to stop hunger dead in its tracks.

———

1   Grill sausages on the Johnsonville® Sizzling Sausage Grill™ (or cook using your favorite method). Cool slightly; dice and set aside.

2   Meanwhile, finely dice potatoes, carrots and onion.

3   In an extra-large skillet, heat canola oil, then add all vegetables, water and thyme. Season with salt and pepper.

4   Mix together, reduce heat to medium and cover. Stir occasionally.

5   Cook over medium heat for 25 to 30 minutes until vegetables are tender.

6   Stir in diced sausage and heat through.

INGREDIENTS

1   (19-ounce) package Johnsonville® Mild Italian Sausage Links

1   large russet potato

1   medium sweet potato

2   large carrots

1   medium onion

1   tablespoon canola oil

2   tablespoons water

½   tablespoon thyme

½   teaspoon salt

¼   teaspoon black pepper

- 1 (19-ounce) package Johnsonville® Chorizo Sausage Links
- 1 pound Brussels sprouts, trimmed and quartered
- 2 tablespoons olive oil

  Salt and pepper, to taste

ROASTED BRUSSELS SPROUTS
WITH CHORIZO

COOK TIME
30
MIN OR LESS

Yes, Brussels sprouts with bacon are delicious, but chorizo takes this dish to a brand-new level.

_____

1 Preheat oven to 400°F.

2 Grill chorizo on the Johnsonville® Sizzling Sausage Grill™ (or cook using your favorite method).

3 While sausage is cooking, toss Brussels sprouts with olive oil, salt and pepper, and spread evenly on a baking sheet; roast for 10 minutes, stirring often.

4 Once sausages are cool enough to handle, cut into ½-inch slices. Toss with roasted Brussels sprouts and serve.

SERVINGS **2** · PREP **20** MIN · COOK **18** MIN

- 2 links Johnsonville® Hot Italian Sausage
- 1 head cauliflower
- 2 tablespoons olive oil
- 2 cloves garlic, minced
- 12 grape tomatoes, halved
- 4 tablespoons basil pesto

  Parmesan cheese, for garnish

CAULIFLOWER RICE
WITH BASIL PESTO
ITALIAN SAUSAGE

COOK TIME **30** MIN OR LESS

Everyone loves pasta and rice, but it's nice to cut carbs whenever you can. Here, cauliflower shares the spotlight in a nutritious supporting role.

1   Grill Italian sausages on the Johnsonville® Sizzling Sausage Grill™ (or cook using your favorite method). Cool slightly; cut into ½-inch slices and set aside.

2   While sausage is cooking, "rice" cauliflower: Cut into large florets, then pulse in a food processor or grate by hand on a box grater.

3   In a medium skillet, heat olive oil over medium heat. Sauté garlic until fragrant, about 2 minutes.

4   Add tomatoes, cauliflower rice and basil pesto, and sauté until tender, about 5 minutes.

5   Add sausage and toss to combine. Garnish with cheese.

3

GAME DAY

INGREDIENTS

- 1 (19-ounce) package Johnsonville® Hot 'n Spicy Brats or Chorizo
- 1 (8-ounce) package cream cheese, room temperature
- 1 (8-ounce) package guacamole
- 1 teaspoon cumin
- 1 teaspoon chili powder
- 1 (16-ounce) can black beans, rinsed and drained
- ½ cup salsa
- 1¼ cups shredded Mexican cheese blend, divided use
- 1 cup chopped tomatoes, divided use
- ¾ cup sliced green onions, divided use
- 1 jalapeño pepper, seeded and chopped

KICK OFF
SAUSAGE DIP

COOK TIME **30** MIN OR LESS

This spicy crowd favorite takes your mother-in-law's 7-layer dip to a whole new level. With just the right amount of kick, you can add this dip to any game day party and people will be begging you to bring it to the next game.

1 Preheat oven to 400°F.

2 Grill brats on the Johnsonville® Sizzling Sausage Grill™ (or cook using your favorite method). Cool slightly; cut into bite-sized pieces and set aside.

3 In a large bowl, combine cream cheese, guacamole, cumin and chili powder.

4 Stir in black beans, salsa, 1 cup of cheese, ½ cup of tomatoes and ½ cup of green onions. Fold in sausage.

5 Spray a deep-dish pie plate with nonstick cooking spray. Spoon sausage mixture into pie plate.

6 Bake for 25 minutes or until golden brown.

7 Remove from oven, and sprinkle with jalapeño and remaining cheese, tomatoes and green onions.

8 Serve warm with tortilla chips.

BRAT CROSTINI

COOK TIME
30
MIN OR LESS

Move over, tomatoes and basil—this crostini combines brats with dill and garlic. Which, in our personal opinion, makes this appetizer far superior.

1 Combine olive oil and garlic; let stand 15 minutes.

2 Grill brats on the Johnsonville® Sizzling Sausage Grill™ (or cook using your favorite method). Cool slightly; cut into ½-inch slices and set aside.

3 Brush olive oil mixture over both sides of each bread slice. Arrange slices on a foil-lined baking sheet. Broil on high for 30 to 60 seconds on each side, or until lightly toasted.

4 Top with brat slices and cheese, then return to oven. Cover and broil for 2 minutes or until cheese is melted.

INGREDIENTS

½ cup olive oil

1 tablespoon garlic, minced

1 (19-ounce) package Johnsonville® Original Brats

1 (1-pound) loaf French bread, cut into ½-inch slices

2½ cups shredded Havarti dill cheese

BRAT POPPERS

COOK TIME
(**30**)
MIN OR LESS

Cheese is overrated. Johnsonville® gives these poppers a real kick by taking the jalapeño heat and adding brats and bacon—no more gooey filler for your poppers.

1 Grill brats on the Johnsonville® Sizzling Sausage Grill™ (or cook using your favorite method).

2 Meanwhile, using a sharp knife, slice ¼ inch off stem end of peppers and discard stem.

3 Using a small knife or vegetable peeler, remove seeds and spines of peppers; discard.

4 Dice sausage into small pieces, and stuff peppers with sausage.

5 Cover stuffed peppers with ⅓ strip of bacon, and secure with a toothpick.

6 Broil on high until evenly roasted and bacon is crisp.

INGREDIENTS

18 jalapeño peppers

1 (19-ounce) package Johnsonville® Original Brats

1 (16-ounce) package bacon, cut into thirds

★ **SAFETY TIP** ★

Wear disposable gloves when cutting hot peppers; the oils can burn your skin. Avoid touching your face.

SERVINGS **4-6** · PREP **30** MIN · COOK **15** MIN

COOK TIME
30
MIN OR LESS

ITALIAN SAUSAGE
CAPRESE SKEWER

1 (19-ounce) package Johnsonville® Hot Italian Sausage Links

24 small wooden skewers or other decorative picks

1 pint cherry tomatoes (24 tomatoes)

1 (2.5-ounce) package fresh basil leaves

1 (16-ounce) tub marinated fresh mozzarella balls

Extra-virgin olive oil

Balsamic syrup*

NOTE: can substitute with balsamic vinegar

Salt and freshly ground black pepper, to taste

* Balsamic syrup is available in finer grocery stores.

What's a great way to add more flavor and deliciousness to a caprese salad? Hot Italian sausage, of course. This quick-and-easy recipe has all of your favorites, too: fresh mozzarella, fresh basil and juicy cherry tomatoes. Then we put it all on a stick because, well, food on a stick just tastes better.

———————

1 Grill Italian sausages on the Johnsonville® Sizzling Sausage Grill™ (or cook using your favorite method). Cool slightly; cut each link into 4 or 5 pieces.

2 Assemble each skewer, alternating the following ingredients: tomatoes, basil, mozzarella and sausage.

3 Arrange skewers on a platter, then drizzle with olive oil and balsamic syrup.

4 Sprinkle with salt and a grinding of fresh black pepper and serve.

SUPER PARTY
BRAT SUB HOAGIE

COOK TIME
30
MIN OR LESS

This is a deliciously big sandwich you can make ahead of game day, then pop in the oven or on the grill right before the game. Sliced brats, peppers, onions and cheese make this a hearty crowd pleaser.

- 1 (19-ounce) package Johnsonville® Original Brats
- 3 tablespoons olive oil
- 1 medium sweet red pepper, sliced
- 1 medium yellow pepper, sliced
- 1 medium green pepper, sliced
- 1 large onion, sliced
- 1 (1-pound) loaf French bread
- 6 slices provolone cheese

1   Grill brats on the Johnsonville® Sizzling Sausage Grill™ (or cook using your favorite method). Cool slightly; slice ¼-inch thick on bias.

2   Preheat oven to 350°F.

3   While the sausage is cooking, heat olive oil in a large skillet, and sauté peppers and onion until tender; set aside.

4   Slice bread lengthwise, and arrange both halves cut-side up on a baking sheet. Layer bottom half with brats, peppers-and-onion mixture and cheese.

5   Place top half on hoagie and bake for 10 minutes or until heated through. Cut hoagie into 6 equal pieces and serve hot.

SWEET POTATO SLIDERS
WITH CHORIZO + AVOCADO SALSA

COOK TIME
30
MIN OR LESS

We may have cut the carbs out of this meal, but the flavors are still bursting. If you're looking for a lighter dish to add to any meal or tailgate, we highly recommend this one.

---

1 Preheat oven to 400°F.

2 Grill sausages on the Johnsonville® Sizzling Sausage Grill™ (or cook using your favorite method). Cool slightly; cut on bias into ½-inch slices.

3 While sausage is cooking, peel sweet potatoes and cut into ¼-inch rounds. Drizzle with olive oil, and season with salt and pepper. Roast until tender, about 20 minutes.

4 Meanwhile, combine avocado, onion, tomato, cilantro and lime juice.

5 To assemble sliders, top roasted potato slices with chorizo and avocado salsa.

INGREDIENTS

- 2 links Johnsonville® Chorizo Sausage
- 2 large sweet potatoes
- 4 tablespoons olive oil
- Salt and pepper, to taste
- 1 avocado, diced
- ¼ cup red onion, diced
- ¼ cup tomato, diced
- 1 tablespoon fresh cilantro, coarsely chopped
- Juice of 2 limes

COOK TIME
30
MIN OR LESS

INGREDIENTS

- 2 links Johnsonville® Original Brats
- 2 tablespoons olive oil
- ½ white cabbage, chopped
- 5 button mushrooms, chopped
- 10 green onions, sliced
- 10 water chestnuts, chopped
- 2 cloves garlic, chopped

STIR FRY SAUCE

- 2 tablespoons soy sauce
- 1 tablespoon rice wine vinegar
- 2 tablespoons brown sugar

  Ramen noodles

  Leaf lettuce

SAUSAGE
LETTUCE WRAPS

We admit that lettuce wraps might be a little messy at a tailgate, but these are worth a little stain on your shirt. These are great to make ahead of time and serve warm or cold.

———

1 Grill brats on the Johnsonville® Sizzling Sausage Grill™ (or cook using your favorite method). Cool slightly; cut into ½-inch slices and set aside.

2 While sausage is cooking, heat olive oil in a pan and add chopped vegetables. Combine all stir-fry sauce ingredients and add to pan. Cook on high for 3 to 4 minutes.

3 Add sausage and cook for 1 minute.

4 Serve with leaf lettuce as a wrap, and garnish with noodles for crunch.

5 Serve with rice wine vinegar or favorite dipping sauce.

JOHNSONVILLE® BRAT HOT TUB

COOK TIME
30
MIN OR LESS

One sure-fire way to make certain all your guests get a piping hot, juicy Johnsonville® Brat is to create a simple bratwurst hot tub.

- 2 (19-ounce) packages Johnsonville® Original Brats
- 2 tablespoons butter
- 1 medium yellow or white onion, sliced
- 2-3 (12-ounce) cans beer of your choice

1 Grill brats on the Johnsonville® Sizzling Sausage Grill™ (or cook using your favorite method).

2 Meanwhile, in a large, heavy-duty disposable foil pan, large saucepan or Dutch oven, melt butter and sauté onion until translucent, about 5 minutes.

3 Add beer to onion and butter, and heat to a simmer.

4 Once brats are thoroughly cooked, add to beer mixture and let simmer for 15 minutes.

ITALIAN SAUSAGE HOT TUB

COOK TIME 30 MIN OR LESS

An easy and sure-fire way to ensure all your guests get a piping hot, juicy Johnsonville® Italian Sausage.

2 (19-ounce) packages Johnsonville® Mild Italian Sausage Links

1 (750 ml) bottle white wine

1 medium green pepper, julienned

1 large sweet red or yellow pepper, julienned

1 (16-ounce) jar cocktail onions, drained

1 (6-ounce) can pitted ripe olives, drained

4 medium cloves garlic, peeled and quartered

1 tablespoon chopped fresh parsley or basil

1 Grill Italian sausage on the Johnsonville® Sizzling Sausage Grill™ (or cook using your favorite method).

2 Meanwhile, in a large, heavy-duty disposable foil pan, large saucepan or Dutch oven, combine wine, peppers, onions, olives, garlic and herbs. Bring to a slow simmer.

3 Once brats are thoroughly cooked, transfer to wine steam bath. Cover and keep warm until ready to serve.

SERVINGS **10** · PREP **10** MIN · COOK **30** MIN

APPLE CIDER
SAUSAGE BATH

COOK TIME
30 MIN OR LESS

Hot apple cider is not just for cool autumn days and hay rides. Use this bath when you want to sweeten the taste of your delicious Johnsonville® brats.

INGREDIENTS

- 2 (19-ounce) packages Johnsonville® Original Brats
- 4 cups apple cider or apple juice
- 2 large onions, sliced
- 1 tablespoon whole cloves
- 1 stick cinnamon

1 Grill brats on the Johnsonville® Sizzling Sausage Grill™ (or cook using your favorite method).

2 Meanwhile, in a large, heavy-duty disposable foil pan, large saucepan or Dutch oven, combine apple cider or juice, onions, cloves and cinnamon; bring to a simmer.

3 Once brats are thoroughly cooked, add to mixture and let simmer for 15 minutes.

ONION + GARLIC
SAUSAGE BATH

COOK TIME
30
MIN OR LESS

Onions and garlic go great with almost everything. Try this bath on Johnsonville® Italian sausages or brats, and give thanks to great combinations.

INGREDIENTS

2 (19-ounce) packages Johnsonville® Italian Sausage Links or Original Brats

1 (32-ounce) carton beef broth

2 large onions, sliced

4 cloves garlic, thinly sliced

1 bunch fresh thyme sprigs

2 bay leaves

1 Grill brats on the Johnsonville® Sizzling Sausage Grill™ (or cook using your favorite method).

2 Meanwhile, in a large, heavy-duty disposable foil pan, large saucepan or Dutch oven, combine broth, onions, garlic, thyme and bay leaves. Bring to a gentle simmer.

3 Once brats are thoroughly cooked, add to broth mixture and let simmer for 15 minutes.

WHISKEY & BLACK PEPPERCORN MUSTARD

- 1 tablespoon black peppercorns
- ½ cup whiskey
- 1 red bell pepper, roasted
- 1 yellow bell pepper, roasted
- 1 green bell pepper, roasted
- 1 medium yellow onion
- ½ cup coarse-ground mustard

———

1. Place peppercorns and whiskey in a medium saucepan. Simmer on low until reduced by half.

2. Cut each bell pepper and the onion in half. Place half of each vegetable in a blender with half of the peppercorns-and-whiskey mixture and mustard, and blend until smooth. Pour mixture into a bowl.

3. Dice remaining vegetable halves. Add to bowl, and mix well to combine. Store refrigerated in an airtight container.

DRUNKEN RED-PEPPER MUSTARD WITH JALAPEÑO

- 1 tablespoon mustard seed
- 2 teaspoons mustard powder
- ½ teaspoon red-pepper flakes
- 1 teaspoon apple cider vinegar
- ½ cup dark beer
- 1 tablespoon chopped fresh chives
- 2 roasted jalapeños in liquid, drained
- 1 (8-ounce) jar coarse-ground mustard

———

1. In a small bowl, combine mustard seed, mustard powder, red-pepper flakes, vinegar and beer. Refrigerate overnight in an airtight container.

2. Heat mixture in a medium saucepan over high heat until reduced by half. Add chives, jalapeños and mustard. Store refrigerated in an airtight container.

AMBER GARLIC MUSTARD WITH DILL

- 1 tablespoon unsalted butter
- 2 cloves garlic, crushed
- 1 tablespoon mustard seed
- ½ cup dark beer
- 1 teaspoon mustard powder
- 1½ teaspoons dried dillweed
- ½ cup horseradish mustard

———

1. Melt butter in a saucepan. Add garlic and mustard seed, and cook over low heat for 3 minutes.

2. Add beer, mustard powder and dillweed, and reduce by half. Mix with mustard, and refrigerate overnight in an airtight container.

AMBER GARLIC MUSTARD WITH DILL

DRUNKEN RED-PEPPER MUSTARD WITH JALAPEÑO

WHISKEY & BLACK PEPPERCORN MUSTARD

SUN-DRIED TOMATO & BASIL MUSTARD WITH FETA

1   tablespoon unsalted butter

2   teaspoons chopped fresh basil

1   clove garlic, crushed

½   cup diced Roma tomatoes

1   cup sun-dried tomatoes, diced

½   cup dark beer

1   (8-ounce) jar course-ground mustard

¼   cup crumbled feta cheese

———

1   Melt butter in a small saucepan over low heat. Add basil, garlic and tomatoes, and cook for 2 minutes.

2   Add beer and reduce by half. Remove from heat and allow to cool slightly.

3   Add mustard and cheese, and mix well to combine. Store refrigerated in an airtight container.

GINGER MUSTARD WITH TOASTED SESAME SEEDS

1   tablespoon butter

½   teaspoon crushed garlic

1   teaspoon fresh ginger, peeled and minced

½   cup dark beer

3   tablespoons sesame seeds, toasted

¾   cup Dijon mustard

1   tablespoon soy sauce

———

1   In a small saucepan, melt butter over low heat. Add garlic and ginger, and sauté for 1 minute.

2   Add beer and sesame seeds; bring to a boil.

3   Reduce heat and simmer, uncovered, until liquid is reduced by half.

4   Remove from heat; whisk in mustard and soy sauce.

5   Cool completely. Store refrigerated in an airtight container.

FRESH TOMATO RELISH

1   pint red grape tomatoes, quartered and diced

1   pint yellow grape tomatoes, quartered and diced

⅓   cup finely chopped red onion

2   teaspoons chopped fresh dill

2   teaspoons seasoned rice vinegar

1   teaspoon canola oil

1   teaspoon sugar

¼   teaspoon sea salt

¼   teaspoon coarsely ground black pepper

———

In a bowl, combine all ingredients and toss gently. Cover and refrigerate for 1 hour.

SUN-DRIED TOMATO & BASIL
MUSTARD WITH FETA

ROASTED SWEET PEPPER & ARTICHOKE RELISH

¼ cup olive oil

2 tablespoons balsamic vinegar

2 tablespoons chopped fresh basil

1 teaspoon sugar

1 teaspoon Dijon mustard

1 clove garlic, minced

Salt and pepper, to taste

2 (7-ounce) jars roasted sweet red peppers, drained and cut into strips

1 (7½-ounce) jar marinated artichoke hearts, drained and coarsely chopped

—————

1 In a bowl, whisk the oil, balsamic vinegar, basil, sugar, mustard, garlic, salt and pepper.

2 Add peppers and artichokes, and toss to coat. Cover and refrigerate for 30 minutes or until ready to serve.

SMOKY BARBECUE RELISH

¼ cup chopped bacon

½ cup chopped onion

½ cup chopped red bell pepper

½ cup chopped yellow bell pepper

½ cup seeded and chopped fresh poblano pepper

3 cloves garlic, minced

1½ cups favorite barbecue sauce

¼ cup chopped fresh cilantro

1 teaspoon lemon juice

—————

1 In a saucepan, cook bacon until crisp. Add onion, peppers and garlic; cook and stir over medium heat until tender.

2 Stir in barbecue sauce. Reduce heat to low and simmer for 15 to 20 minutes.

3 Remove from heat; stir in cilantro and lemon juice.

TART CRANBERRY & ONION RELISH

1 (10-ounce) package dried cranberries

2 cups chopped onion

¼ cup cider vinegar

2 tablespoons sugar

1 (12-ounce) jar red currant jelly

—————

1 In a saucepan, combine cranberries, onion, vinegar and sugar.

2 Bring to a boil. Reduce heat to low; cover and simmer until onion is tender. Remove from heat and stir in jelly.

3 Cover and refrigerate for 30 minutes or until ready to serve.

SWEET & SOUR CUCUMBER & ONION RELISH

3 teaspoons salt

1 cup sugar

½ cup white vinegar

2 cucumbers, seeded and sliced thin

1 onion, sliced thin

---

1 In a saucepan, combine salt, sugar and vinegar. Heat over medium heat, stirring until salt and sugar are dissolved.

2 Remove from heat and allow to cool.

3 In a bowl, toss cucumbers and onion. Add vinegar mixture.

4 Cover and refrigerate overnight.

SWEET & SOUR CUCUMBER & ONION RELISH

4

SOUPS

INGREDIENTS

- 1 (19-ounce) package Johnsonville® Italian Sausage Links
- 1 tablespoon olive oil
- 3 medium carrots, chopped (1½ cups)
- 1 medium onion, chopped (1½ cups)
- 2 celery stalks, chopped (1 cup)
- 4 cloves garlic, minced
- 3 (14.5-ounce) cans low-sodium chicken broth
- 1 cup water
- 1 tablespoon dried parsley
- 1 teaspoon dried rosemary, crushed
- ½ teaspoon dried oregano

  Salt and freshly ground black pepper, to taste

- 6 ounces kale, thick ribs removed, chopped (about 1½ bunches), or 5 ounces if using pre-cut
- 2 (14.5-ounce) cans cannellini beans, drained and rinsed

  Shredded Parmesan cheese, for serving

KALE, WHITE BEAN & SAUSAGE SOUP

COOK TIME
30
MIN OR LESS

This herbaceous soup is great year-round. Hearty enough to warm you in the winter and refreshing enough to enjoy in the summer, it's full of flavor and nutrition.

1 Grill Italian sausages on the Johnsonville® Sizzling Sausage Grill™ (or cook using your favorite method). Cool slightly; cut into ½-inch slices and set aside.

2 While sausage is cooking, heat olive oil in a large pot over medium heat. Add carrots, onion and celery, and sauté for 3 minutes, taking care to scrape bottom of pan to loosen any browned bits. Add garlic and sauté for 1 more minute.

3 Stir in chicken broth, water, parsley, rosemary and oregano; season with salt and pepper. Bring to a boil over medium-high heat, and allow to gently boil for 10 minutes.

4 Add kale and allow to boil for 10 more minutes, until kale and veggies are tender. Stir in cooked sausage and cannellini beans. **NOTE:** *You can add more broth at this point to thin, if desired.*

5 Serve warm, and top each serving with cheese.

- 1 (19-ounce) package Johnsonville® Mild or Hot Italian Sausage Links
- 2 tablespoons olive oil
- 5 medium carrots, sliced
- 1 large onion, chopped
- 3 celery ribs, chopped
- 2 cartons (32 ounces each) chicken broth
- 2 medium zucchini, sliced
- 1 medium summer squash, sliced
- 2 cups kale, thinly sliced
- 1 pint cherry tomatoes, halved
- ½ teaspoon pepper

FARMER'S MARKET
SAUSAGE SOUP

COOK TIME
30
MIN OR LESS

For a bountiful soup reminiscent of the day's harvest, this recipe brings together a wide range of fresh veggies to create a balanced, light taste: carrots, onion, celery, zucchini, kale and summer squash.

1 Grill Italian sausages on the Johnsonville® Sizzling Sausage Grill™ (or cook using your favorite method). Cool slightly; cut into ½-inch slices and set aside.

2 Meanwhile, in a soup pot, heat olive oil and sauté carrots, onion and celery until vegetables are tender, about 10 minutes.

3 Stir in sausage, broth, zucchini, squash, kale, tomatoes and pepper; bring to a boil.

4 Reduce heat and simmer for 10 minutes. Serve warm.

INGREDIENTS

- 1 (19-ounce) package Johnsonville® Hot Italian Sausage Links
- 3 tablespoons butter
- 2 cups onions, chopped
- 5 tablespoons unbleached flour
- 6 cups chicken stock (48 ounces)
- 2 large potatoes, peeled and cut into ¼-inch dice
- 1½ cups half-and-half (or light cream)
- 3 cups corn kernels, fresh or frozen
- 1 teaspoon fresh thyme leaves, chopped, or ½ teaspoon, dried
  Salt, to taste
- 1 large red bell pepper, cut into ¼-inch dice
- 3 green onions, cut into ¼-inch slices
- 1 tablespoon Italian parsley, chopped

CORN & POTATO
CHOWDER
WITH HOT ITALIAN SAUSAGE

We love a good chowder, but it always feels like it's missing something: the meat. We remedy that in this dish by adding hot Italian sausage, which provides protein and spiciness.

1   Grill Italian sausages on the Johnsonville® Sizzling Sausage Grill™ (or cook using your favorite method). Remove from heat and allow sausage to cool.

2   In a large soup pot, melt butter and add onions; cook until softened, about 10 minutes.

3   Add flour to onions, stirring together, and cook for 3 more minutes.

4   Add stock, stirring frequently, and bring to a gentle boil. Reduce heat to medium-low, then add potatoes and stir to combine.

5   Continue cooking over medium-low heat until potatoes are tender, about 10 to 15 more minutes.

6   Add half-and-half, corn, thyme and salt. Cook for 5 to 7 more minutes, stirring occasionally and being careful not to allow it to boil.

7   Meanwhile, transfer cooled sausage to a cutting board and cut in half lengthwise and then into ¼-inch half-moon slices. Add sausage, bell pepper and green onions to soup pot; simmer gently for 5 to 10 more minutes.

8   Serve immediately, or reheat when ready to serve. Top with a sprinkling of fresh Italian parsley. **NOTE**: This can be made a day ahead and stored in refrigerator.

HEARTY
MINESTRONE

COOK TIME
30
MIN OR LESS

With a soup this rich and hearty, you won't need the sandwich. Though we won't fault you for adding one.

---

1   Grill Italian sausages on the Johnsonville® Sizzling Sausage Grill™ (or cook using your favorite method). Cool slightly; cut into ½-inch slices and set aside.

2   Meanwhile, in a large stockpot, sauté bell pepper, onion and celery for 5 minutes, or until vegetables are tender.

3   Add all remaining ingredients and bring to a boil.

4   Reduce heat to low; cover and simmer for 20 to 25 minutes, or until pasta is tender. Serve warm.

INGREDIENTS

1   (19-ounce) package Johnsonville® Hot Italian Sausage Links

1   medium red bell pepper, chopped

1   medium onion, chopped

1   cup celery, chopped

4   cups beef broth

2   cups uncooked small shell pasta

1   (15.5-ounce) can great northern beans, rinsed and drained

1   (14.5-ounce) can whole tomatoes, chopped

1   medium zucchini, chopped

1   medium potato, peeled and chopped

1   cup red wine

½   teaspoon dried oregano

½   teaspoon dried basil

½   teaspoon salt

½   teaspoon pepper

TOUCHDOWN
ITALIAN
SAUSAGE CHILI

Warm, hearty and full of sausage, this is one chili that scores big points with the crowd. Make it the day before for easy serving and even more flavor.

1   Grill Italian sausages on the Johnsonville® Sizzling Sausage Grill™ (or cook using your favorite method). Cool slightly; cut into half-moon slices and set aside.

2   In a soup kettle, heat olive oil and sauté onion, celery, sweet pepper and garlic until tender.

3   Add sausage and all remaining ingredients; bring to a boil.

4   Reduce heat; cover and simmer for 20 minutes, or until flavors are blended. Serve warm.

INGREDIENTS

1   (19-ounce) package Johnsonville® Mild or Hot Italian Sausage Links

3   tablespoons olive oil

1   cup chopped onion

3   celery ribs, cut into ½-inch pieces

1   large sweet red pepper, cut into 1-inch pieces

1   tablespoon minced garlic

1   large yellow pepper, cut into 1-inch pieces

1   large green pepper, cut into 1-inch pieces

3   (14½-ounce) cans Italian recipe stewed tomatoes

1   (16-ounce) can dark red kidney beans, rinsed and drained

1   (15-ounce) can butter beans, rinsed and drained

1   (6-ounce) can tomato paste

¾   cup sliced black olives

¼   cup cream sherry (optional)

1   tablespoon chopped fresh basil

1½   teaspoons baking cocoa

½-1 teaspoon pepper

MVP CHILI

While chili aficionados will argue over what true chili really is, we think this recipe brings together many of the quintessential, well-loved chili ingredients. So let them debate while you devour this version.

----

2 (19-ounce) packages Johnsonville® Hot Italian Sausage Links (use mild links for a less spicy chili)

1 tablespoon olive oil

1 large onion, diced

3 cloves garlic, minced

2 tablespoons chili powder (use mild chili powder for a less spicy chili)

¼ teaspoon cumin

1 (12-ounce) bottle dark beer (can substitute light beer or 1 cup beef stock)

1 (28-ounce) can crushed tomatoes

2 tablespoons tomato paste

Salt and pepper, to taste

1 (15.5-ounce) can black beans

1 (15.5-ounce) can red kidney beans

1½ cups corn, frozen or fresh off the cob

1   Grill Italian sausages on the Johnsonville® Sizzling Sausage Grill™ (or cook using your favorite method). Cool slightly; cut into ¼-inch slices and set aside.

2   Meanwhile, in a large skillet, heat olive oil and sauté onion, garlic, chili powder and cumin until onion softens, about 5 minutes.

3   Add beer and allow to simmer for 5 more minutes, taking care to scrape bottom of pan to loosen any browned bits.

4   Stir in tomatoes and tomato paste, and allow to simmer, uncovered, for 10 to 15 more minutes over medium-low heat, stirring occasionally.

5   Season with salt and pepper.

6   Stir in beans, corn and sausage. Bring to a simmer and serve. **NOTE:** This can be made a day ahead and stored in refrigerator.

ITALIAN WEDDING SOUP

This traditional soup is a favorite in many restaurants, but it's easy to make at home too. The sausage flavor really comes through in this soup, as it pairs nicely with the more subtle flavors of orzo, celery, carrots and spinach.

---

1 Grill Italian sausages on the Johnsonville® Sizzling Sausage Grill™ (or cook using your favorite method). Cool slightly; cut into ¼-inch slices and set aside.

2 Meanwhile, in a medium pan, cook orzo al dente, according to package directions, then drain and set aside.

3 In a large pot, heat olive oil and sauté onion, thyme and sage. When onion starts to turn a golden color, add garlic, carrot and celery, and cook for about 5 minutes, stirring occasionally.

4 In the same pot with the vegetables, add sausage, chicken stock and bay leaf. Simmer gently, being careful not to bring to a boil, until vegetables are tender.

5 Add orzo and spinach, and stir to combine.

   NOTE: Adding spinach right before serving will help it maintain its rich green color.

6 Garnish soup bowls with cheese and serve.

INGREDIENTS

- 1 (19-ounce) package Johnsonville® Mild Italian Sausage Links
- 8 ounces orzo pasta
- 2 tablespoons extra-virgin olive oil
- 1 medium onion, finely diced
- 1 teaspoon dried or fresh thyme
- 1 teaspoon dried sage leaves
- 2 cloves garlic, finely minced
- 1 medium carrot, finely chopped
- 1 stalk celery, finely chopped
- 8 cups chicken stock
- 1 bay leaf
- 1 cup spinach, roughly chopped
- ⅓ cup shredded Parmesan cheese

SAUSAGE &
SWEET POTATO SOUP

Chorizo and sweet potatoes are a match made in soup heaven. Plus, we love the chunkiness of this rough-cut soup. Every spoonful is as colorful as it is flavorful.

---

1   Grill chorizo on the Johnsonville® Sizzling Sausage Grill™ (or cook using your favorite method). Cool slightly; cut into ½-inch slices and set aside.

2   Meanwhile, in a large soup pot, heat olive oil and sauté bell pepper, onion and celery until tender, about 10 minutes. Sprinkle with basil, salt and pepper; toss to coat.

3   Stir in sausage, vegetable broth, tomatoes, zucchini and sweet potatoes; bring to a boil. Reduce heat and simmer for 40 minutes, or until vegetables are tender.

INGREDIENTS

- 1 (19-ounce) package Johnsonville® Chorizo Sausage Links
- 2 tablespoons olive oil
- 1 medium red bell pepper, chopped
- 1 medium onion, chopped
- 1 cup celery, chopped
- ½ teaspoon dried basil
- ½ teaspoon salt
- ½ teaspoon pepper
- 4 cups vegetable broth
- 1 (14.5-ounce) can whole tomatoes, chopped
- 1 medium zucchini, chopped
- 2 medium sweet potatoes, peeled and chopped

S

SANDWICHES

INGREDIENTS

SAUCE

1 cup sour cream

½ medium cucumber, peeled, seeded and finely chopped

2 cloves garlic, minced

2 teaspoons chopped fresh parsley

¼ teaspoon salt

¼ teaspoon cracked black pepper (optional)

HOAGIE

1 (19-ounce) package Johnsonville® Original Brats

1 (1-pound) loaf French bread

1 small onion, thinly sliced

1 medium tomato, thinly sliced

GYRO BRAT
HOAGIE

All the gyro taste you love is baked into a hearty hoagie roll and stuffed with brats, onions and a tasty sauce—all the flavor without the mess. It's also an excellent use for pregame brat fry leftovers. Make it ahead of time, then bake it in the oven or on the grill at the tailgate.

———

1 Preheat oven to 350°F.

2 In a bowl, combine sauce ingredients. Cover and refrigerate until ready to serve.

3 Grill brats on the Johnsonville® Sizzling Sausage Grill™ (or cook using your favorite method). Cool slightly; slice ¼-inch thick on bias.

4 Meanwhile, slice bread lengthwise, and arrange both halves cut-side up on a baking sheet.

5 Arrange brat slices on bottom half of bread.

6 Bake for 10 minutes or until bread is lightly browned. Remove from oven. Top with sauce, onion and tomato. Place top half of bread on hoagie; cut and serve.

OKTOBERFEST
HOAGIE

COOK TIME
30
MIN OR LESS

This sandwich—loaded with brats, turkey, ham and bacon—is for the serious carnivore. Add some tangy horseradish sauce and a delicious German beer, and pretend you're at Oktoberfest. *Guten Appetit!*

1   Grill brat on the Johnsonville® Sizzling Sausage Grill™ (or cook using your favorite method).

2   Spread horseradish sauce on inside of roll.

3   Cut brat in half lengthwise and place on roll.

4   Arrange remaining ingredients on top of brat.

5   Serve with chips, french fries or coleslaw.

INGREDIENTS

1   link Johnsonville® Original Brat

2   tablespoons horseradish sauce (1 tablespoon mayo and 1 tablespoon horseradish mixed together)

1   hoagie roll, split in half lengthwise

1   ounce smoked turkey, thinly sliced

1   ounce fully cooked ham, thinly sliced

1   medium tomato, sliced

2   thin slices provolone cheese

2   slices bacon, cooked crisp

1   small onion, sliced

1   dill pickle, sliced

INGREDIENTS

1 (19-ounce) package Johnsonville® Original Brats

1 large onion, sliced

1 teaspoon butter

⅓ cup Thousand Island dressing

⅓ cup coarse ground mustard

1 (1-pound) loaf French bread

1 (14-ounce) can sauerkraut, drained

12 thin slices Swiss cheese

REUBEN BRAT
HOAGIE

Grilled and sliced Johnsonville® sausage, Swiss cheese and Thousand Island dressing combine on a hearty hoagie roll for the perfect game-day crowd pleaser. Add chips and a pickle, and watch the fans come running at halftime.

1 Preheat oven to 350°F.

2 Grill brats on the Johnsonville® Sizzling Sausage Grill™ (or cook using your favorite method). Cool slightly; slice ¼-inch thick on bias.

3 While sausage is cooking, sauté onion in butter until tender; set aside. In a small bowl, combine dressing and mustard.

4 Slice bread lengthwise, and arrange both halves cut-side up on a baking sheet.

5 Spread dressing mixture on bottom half of bread. Layer with 6 slices of cheese, brats, onion, sauerkraut and remaining cheese.

6 Bake for 10 minutes or until cheese is melted. Cut hoagie and serve hot.

BRAT & PEPPER
HOAGIE

COOK TIME
30
MIN OR LESS

This is a gigantic sandwich you can make a day ahead of game day, then pop in the oven right before the game. Sliced brats, peppers, onions and cheese make this a hearty crowd pleaser that's even great warmed on the grill at halftime.

---

1   Preheat oven to 350°F.

2   Grill brats on the Johnsonville® Sizzling Sausage Grill™ (or cook using your favorite method). Let cool slightly; cut into ¼-inch bias slices.

3   In a skillet, sauté peppers and onion in olive oil until tender; set aside.

4   Slice bread lengthwise, and arrange both halves cut-side up on a baking sheet. Layer bottom half of bread with brats, pepper-and-onion mixture and provolone cheese.

5   Place top half of bread on hoagie and bake for 10 minutes, or until heated through. Cut hoagie and serve hot.

1   (19-ounce) package Johnsonville® Original Brats

1   medium sweet red pepper, sliced

1   medium yellow pepper, sliced

1   medium green pepper, sliced

1   large onion, sliced

3   tablespoons olive oil

2   loaves baguette-style French bread

6   slices provolone cheese

ITALIAN
SAUSAGE MELT

COOK TIME
30
MIN OR LESS

We like to think of this as the ultimate grilled cheese, since we added—you guessed it—sausage. A good loaf of focaccia and perfectly aged balsamic take this sandwich over the top.

---

1   Grill sausages on the Johnsonville® Sizzling Sausage Grill™ (or cook using your favorite method). Cool slightly; slice in half lengthwise.

2   While sausage is cooking, brush both sides of cheese and tomato slices with balsamic reduction; sprinkle tomatoes with garlic salt and pepper.

3   Slice bread in half lengthwise; replace top and cut into quarters.

4   Layer tomatoes, cheese, basil and sausage on bottom half of each bread quarter; top with bread tops.

5   Spread butter on outside of bread. Grill in a skillet until cheese is melted.

INGREDIENTS

1   (19-ounce) package Johnsonville® Sweet or Mild Italian Sausage Links

8   slices fresh mozzarella

2   tomatoes, sliced

¼   cup balsamic reduction

Garlic salt and pepper, to taste

1   (14-ounce) round loaf focaccia bread

Basil leaves

2   tablespoons butter, melted

INGREDIENTS

- 1 (19-ounce) package Johnsonville® Original Brats
- 1 large onion, cut into ¼-inch-thick slices
- 1 medium green pepper
- 1 medium sweet red pepper
- 1 medium sweet yellow pepper
- 1-2 jalapeño peppers (optional)
- 2 tablespoons olive oil
- 1 tablespoon fresh cracked pepper
- 5 hoagie rolls, split in half lengthwise

SPICY
CRACKED BLACK PEPPER BRATS

We add four different kinds of peppers to the brats in this recipe. It's quick and easy, and bursting with flavor.

1 Grill brats on the Johnsonville® Sizzling Sausage Grill™ (or cook using your favorite method).

2 Meanwhile, julienne onion and peppers.

3 Sauté onion and peppers in olive oil until soft.

4 Add cracked pepper to onion-and-pepper mixture; toss gently.

5 Place 1 brat in each roll. Top with pepper-and-onion mixture. Serve hot.

INGREDIENTS

- 1 (19-ounce) package Johnsonville® Original Brats
- 1 medium sweet red pepper, sliced
- 1 medium yellow pepper, sliced
- 1 medium green pepper, sliced
- 1 large onion, sliced
- 3 tablespoons olive oil
- ¾ cup Cheez Whiz® cheese sauce
- 5 hoagie rolls, split in half lengthwise

PHILLY BRATS

COOK TIME **30** MIN OR LESS

A new take on a traditional favorite, these brats are so delicious that we think even die-hard Philadelphians will love them.

1   Grill brats on the Johnsonville® Sizzling Sausage Grill™ (or cook using your favorite method).

2   While sausage is cooking, sauté peppers and onion in olive oil until tender.

3   Place 1 brat in each roll. Top with peppers, onions and cheese sauce. Serve hot.

6

QUICK 'N' EASY
ENTRÉES

INGREDIENTS

CHEDDAR BRAT
MAC & CHEESE

Standard mac and cheese gets a flavorful upgrade with the addition of cheddar brats—and a jar of queso dip. Sign us up.

INGREDIENTS

- 1 (19-ounce) package Johnsonville® Cheddar Brats
- 1 (16-ounce) package elbow macaroni
- 1 (23-ounce) jar salsa con queso
- 1 cup sharp cheddar cheese, cubed
- ½ cup water
- 1 teaspoon ground cumin
- ⅛ teaspoon cayenne pepper
- ¾ cup shredded pepper Jack cheese
- 3 green onions, sliced (optional)

1 Grill brats on the Johnsonville® Sizzling Sausage Grill™ (or cook using your favorite method). Cool slightly; cut into ½-inch slices.

2 While sausage is cooking, cook macaroni according to package directions for firm pasta.

3 In a large saucepan, combine the salsa con queso, cheddar cheese, water, cumin and cayenne.

4 Stir in brats and macaroni. Sprinkle with pepper Jack cheese and green onions.

NEW ORLEANS
JAMBALAYA

Jambalaya can't get much better than this, especially since it takes less than 30 minutes to make.

1 Grill brats on the Johnsonville® Sizzling Sausage Grill™ (or cook using your favorite method). Cool slightly; cut into ½-inch half-moon slices and set aside.

2 While sausage is cooking, combine tomatoes with green chilies, stewed tomatoes, onion, green pepper and water in a large saucepan.

3 Bring to a boil. Add rice and reduce heat.

4 Cover and simmer for 20 to 25 minutes or until rice is tender.

5 Stir in sliced sausage and heat through.

INGREDIENTS

1 (19-ounce) package Johnsonville® Hot 'n Spicy Brats

1 (14.5-ounce) can diced tomatoes with green chilies

1 (14.5-ounce) can stewed tomatoes

1 large onion, chopped

1 green pepper, chopped

1 cup water

¾ cup rice

FIRESTORM
BURRITO

COOK TIME **30** MIN OR LESS

Hot 'n Spicy brats give this Mexican-inspired dish some serious kick. The lime-and-garlic salsa adds an even deeper flavor profile.

_____

1 Mix together sour cream, seasoning and cilantro; set aside.

2 Grill brats on the Johnsonville® Sizzling Sausage Grill™ (or cook using your favorite method); keep warm.

3 While sausage is cooking, heat tortillas; spread about 2 tablespoons of sour cream sauce onto each tortilla, then top with 2 tablespoons of salsa.

4 Layer each tortilla with 1 brat and 1 tablespoon each of green pepper, red pepper, tomato and onions.

5 Sprinkle 1 ounce of shredded cheese on top, and roll up burrito-style.

★ TIP ★

To keep the sausage warm while finishing the other elements of this dish, keep the grill lid shut until it's time to serve.

INGREDIENTS

1 cup sour cream

2½ teaspoons roasted chipotle and onion seasoning

1 tablespoon cilantro, freshly chopped

1 (19-ounce) package Johnsonville® Hot 'n Spicy Brats

1 package 10- to 12-inch flour tortillas

1 jar lime-and-garlic salsa

1 green pepper, finely diced

1 red pepper, finely diced

1 tomato, diced

1 bunch green onions, sliced

1 red onion, sliced

8 ounces shredded pepper Jack cheese

INGREDIENTS

- 1 (19-ounce) package Johnsonville® Mild Italian Sausage Links
- 2 tablespoons olive oil
- 2 cloves garlic, crushed
- 1 small red pepper, julienned
- 1 small green pepper, julienned
- 1 small yellow pepper, julienned
- 1 small onion, julienned
- ½ teaspoon dried basil
- 1 (14.5-ounce) can Italian diced tomatoes

  Salt and pepper, to taste

ITALIAN SAUSAGE & PEPPER
SKILLET

COOK TIME 30 MIN OR LESS

An easy and authentic Italian dish your whole family will crave any night of the week.

———

1 Grill Italian sausages on the Johnsonville® Sizzling Sausage Grill™ (or cook using your favorite method). Slice ¼ inch thick on bias and set aside.

2 While sausage is cooking, add olive oil and garlic to a large saucepan, and sauté for about 30 seconds.

3 Add peppers and onion, and sauté for 5 more minutes or until crisp-tender.

4 Add basil, tomatoes and sausage. Heat through, and season with salt and pepper.

| SERVINGS 4-6 | ⏱ PREP 30 MIN | ⏱ COOK 60 MIN |

INGREDIENTS

- ¾ cup dry quinoa (can substitute brown rice or couscous)
- 1 (19-ounce) package Johnsonville® Italian Sausage Links
- 1 tablespoon olive oil
- 1 small red onion, finely chopped
- 1 medium red bell pepper, chopped into ¼-inch cubes
- 3 plum tomatoes, chopped
- 4 ounces mushrooms, chopped
- 2 tablespoons fresh parsley, chopped
- 1 teaspoon paprika
- ½ cup grated Parmesan cheese
- ½ teaspoon salt
- 6 to 7 medium bell peppers, tops removed, cored and seeded
- ¼ cup toasted sliced almonds* (optional)

★ TIP ★

Toast almonds in a dry skillet over medium heat, stirring and shaking pan constantly, for 3 to 4 minutes or until golden. Immediately transfer to a bowl and let cool.

ITALIAN SAUSAGE & QUINOA
STUFFED PEPPERS

Quinoa is a delicious way to add a healthy element without losing any delectability. Packed with protein and essential nutrients, this is a great go-to meal for busy weekdays.

———

1 Cook quinoa according to package directions (yields 1½ cups).

2 Grill Italian sausages on the Johnsonville® Sizzling Sausage Grill™ (or cook using your favorite method). Cool slightly; small dice and set aside.

3 While sausage is cooking, heat olive oil in a large skillet, and sauté chopped onion and bell pepper over medium heat for 5 minutes or until softened.

4 Add tomatoes and mushrooms; sauté for 5 more minutes.

5 Remove from heat, then add parsley, cooked quinoa, paprika, sausage and cheese. Stir to combine.

6 Preheat oven to 350°F.

7 Stuff bell peppers with sausage mixture, dividing equally and gently packing the mixture down. Arrange upright in a prepared baking dish.

8 Cover and bake for about 1 hour or until peppers are tender. If desired, serve topped with a sprinkling of toasted almonds.

TASTY
SAUSAGE TACO

COOK TIME
30
MIN OR LESS

Taco night is a favorite in many households. The toppings in this dish might be listed as optional, but we think they should be mandatory.

1 Grill brats or chorizo on the Johnsonville® Sizzling Sausage Grill™ (or cook using your favorite method). Let cool slightly; cut into quarters lengthwise, then dice.

2 Divide sausage evenly among taco shells. Garnish with your favorite toppings.

INGREDIENTS

1 (19-ounce) package Johnsonville® Brats or Chorizo Sausage Links

10 hard-shell tacos

OPTIONAL TOPPINGS

Lettuce, shredded

Guacamole

Tomatoes, chopped

Jalapeños, seeded and chopped

Black olives, chopped

Green onions, chopped

Sour cream

Red onion, chopped

Cilantro, chopped

SAUSAGE ENCHILADAS

COOK TIME
30
MIN OR LESS

Another quick-and-easy meal, perfect for families on the go. Keep these ingredients on hand to eliminate the midweek dinnertime blahs.

---

1 Grill brats on the Johnsonville® Sizzling Sausage Grill™ (or cook using your favorite method). Cool slightly; cut into ½-inch slices and set aside.

2 Preheat oven to 350°F.

3 Divide sausage and 4 ounces of cheese equally among tortillas. Roll up each tortilla burrito-style.

4 Cover tortillas with enchilada sauce and remaining cheese.

5 Bake in a greased baking dish for 10 minutes or until cheese is melted.

INGREDIENTS

1 (19-ounce) package Johnsonville® Original Brats

4 large soft flour tortillas

8 ounces shredded Monterey Jack cheese, divided

1 (14-ounce) can enchilada sauce

Onion, chopped, for garnish

Sour cream, for garnish

INGREDIENTS

- 3 links Johnsonville® Mild or Hot Italian Sausage
- 3 tablespoons olive oil
- 4 cloves garlic, minced
- 1 sweet onion, diced
- 1 teaspoon dried thyme
- 1 teaspoon dried basil
- 1 pint cherry or grape tomatoes
- 4 large zucchinis, sliced into noodles*

  Freshly grated Parmesan cheese

  Salt and pepper, to taste

★ TIP ★

You can use a spiralizer, julienne peeler or mandoline to make zucchini noodles.

ITALIAN SAUSAGE & ZUCCHINI
NOODLE SKILLET

COOK TIME
30
MIN OR LESS

Try this recipe for a light, refreshing take on Italian fare. We like using a spiralizer to make the zucchini noodles—it's just so fun—but if you don't have one, a mandoline or julienne peeler will do just fine.

1 Grill Italian sausages on the Johnsonville® Sizzling Sausage Grill™ (or cook using your favorite method). Cool slightly; cut into ½-inch slices and set aside.

2 While sausage is cooking, heat olive oil in a large skillet over medium heat. Add garlic and sauté until fragrant, about 2 minutes. Add onion and sauté until translucent, about 10 minutes.

3 Add thyme, basil and tomatoes, and cook for 10 more minutes until tomatoes begin to blister.

4 Add sausage and zucchini noodles to skillet, and toss to combine with tomato mixture. Sauté for 1 to 3 minutes until zucchini noodles are cooked to your liking.

5 Garnish with shredded Parmesan, and season with salt and pepper.

SAUSAGE, PEPPERS &
SPAGHETTI
SQUASH

COOK TIME
30
MIN OR LESS

Spaghetti squash will likely become one of your favorite foods after tasting this quick and easy dish.

⎯⎯⎯⎯⎯⎯⎯

1 Grill Italian sausages on the Johnsonville® Sizzling Sausage Grill™ (or cook using your favorite method). Cool slightly; cut into ½-inch slices and set aside.

2 While sausage is cooking, heat olive oil in a large skillet and sauté fennel, onion, peppers and garlic until tender.

3 Add tomatoes, sausage and 3 tablespoons of sherry; cook and stir until heated through.

4 Season with salt and pepper. Just before serving, stir in remaining sherry.

5 Serve hot over spaghetti squash.

INGREDIENTS

1 (19-ounce) package Johnsonville® Sweet Italian Sausage Links

2 tablespoons olive oil

1½ cups fresh fennel, sliced

½ cup green onion, diced

½ cup sweet red pepper, diced

½ cup green pepper, diced

2 tablespoons garlic, minced

1 cup fresh tomatoes, diced

6 tablespoons cooking sherry, divided

Salt and pepper, to taste

3 cups cooked spaghetti squash

ZUCCHINI LASAGNA ROLLS
WITH HOT ITALIAN SAUSAGE

This is a fun take on traditional lasagna that will impress your family or guests. It's pretty, low-carb and delicious. What more could you ask for?

1 Preheat oven to 375°F.

2 Grill Italian sausages on the Johnsonville® Sizzling Sausage Grill™ (or cook using your favorite method). Cool slightly; dice and set aside.

3 While sausage is cooking, mix together ricotta cheese, 8 ounces of mozzarella, oregano and basil.

4 To assemble rolls, spread equal parts ricotta mixture and tomato sauce on each zucchini slice; top with diced sausage. Roll and place in a baking dish, seam-side down.

5 Top zucchini rolls with remaining tomato sauce; sprinkle with remaining mozzarella.

6 Bake, covered, for about 40 minutes until bubbly. Uncover and continue cooking for about 5 more minutes.

7 Let stand 5 minutes, sprinkle with Parmesan and serve.

INGREDIENTS

1 (19-ounce) package Johnsonville® Hot Italian Sausage Links

15 ounces part-skim ricotta cheese

16 ounces shredded part-skim mozzarella cheese, divided

2 tablespoons fresh oregano, chopped

2 tablespoons fresh basil, chopped

4 cups tomato sauce

4 medium zucchini, sliced ⅛ inch thick

Freshly grated Parmesan cheese

SERVINGS **5-6** | PREP **5** MIN | COOK **20** MIN

SAUSAGE BROCCOLI
STIR FRY

Stir fry is one of our favorite meals, especially with fresh ginger. Here we use broccoli but you can, of course, substitute any of your favorite veggies.

---

1 Grill brats on the Johnsonville® Sizzling Sausage Grill™ (or cook using your favorite method). Cool slightly; cut into ½-inch slices and set aside.

2 While sausage is cooking, heat sesame oil in a wok or large skillet over medium-high heat. Sauté ginger and garlic until fragrant, about 2 minutes.

3 Add broccoli, mushrooms, water and teriyaki, oyster or plum sauce; cook and stir for 3 to 4 minutes or until broccoli is crisp-tender. Add sausage and toss to combine.

4 Serve over brown rice or quinoa. Top with cashew halves, if desired.

FARMERS' MARKET
SAUSAGE BAKE

This dish proves that simple is delicious. No need for sauces or fancy techniques. This go-to recipe is as easy as it is flavorful.

_____

1   Grill brats on the Johnsonville® Sizzling Sausage Grill™ (or cook using your favorite method). Cool slightly; cut into ½-inch slices and set aside.

2   Preheat oven to 400°F.

3   While sausage is cooking, lightly toss vegetables with olive oil and black pepper.

4   Spoon vegetable mixture into a greased, shallow 3-quart baking dish.

5   Bake, covered, for 15 minutes.

6   Add sliced sausage and bake another 5 minutes until heated through.

INGREDIENTS

- 1 (19-ounce) package Johnsonville® Cheddar Brats
- 2 medium zucchini, cut into chunks
- 1 yellow summer squash, cut into chunks
- 1 small onion, coarsely chopped
- 2 carrots, peeled and sliced
- 1 small sweet red bell pepper, coarsely chopped
- 1 tablespoon olive oil
- ¼ teaspoon coarsely ground pepper

INGREDIENTS

- 1 (19-ounce) package Johnsonville® Chorizo Sausage Links
- 2 tablespoons olive oil
- 1 green pepper, sliced
- 1 red pepper, sliced
- 1 onion, sliced
- 1 can low-fat refried black beans, heated
- 8 corn or wheat tortillas, or lettuce cups
- ½ cup shredded Monterey Jack cheese
- 1 avocado
- ½ cup sour cream

CHORIZO FAJITAS

COOK TIME 30 MIN OR LESS

Fajitas are already bursting with flavor, but we add even more by using chorizo instead of chicken or steak. Cut the carbs by substituting lettuce cups for tortillas.

————

1 Grill chorizo on the Johnsonville® Sizzling Sausage Grill™ (or cook using your favorite method). Cool slightly; cut into ½-inch slices and set aside.

2 While sausage is cooking, heat olive oil in a large skillet, and sauté peppers and onion until peppers are lightly browned and tender.

3 Spread desired amount of black beans onto each tortilla or lettuce cup.

4 Top with sausage, peppers and onion, and garnish with cheese, avocado and sour cream, according to taste.

KALE & SAUSAGE BUTTERNUT
NOODLE SKILLET

COOK TIME
30
MIN OR LESS

Kale has become so popular—and we're glad. We love using it whenever possible. It's versatile and adds great color to this dish.

———

1   Preheat oven to 400°F.

2   Toss squash noodles with 2 tablespoons of olive oil in a baking dish; roast for 20 minutes.

3   While the noodles are roasting, grill Italian sausages on the Johnsonville® Sizzling Sausage Grill™ (or cook using your favorite method). Cool slightly; cut into ½-inch slices and set aside.

4   In a large skillet, heat remaining olive oil over medium heat. Add garlic and sauté until fragrant, about 2 minutes.

5   Add roasted noodles, broth and kale, and cook until broth is absorbed and kale is tender, about 5 minutes.

6   Add sausage and toss to combine.

7   Garnish with cheese.

INGREDIENTS

2   butternut squash, sliced into noodles★

4   tablespoons olive oil, divided

3   links Johnsonville® Mild or Hot Italian Sausage

2   cloves garlic, minced

½   cup vegetable broth

1   bunch kale, ribs removed, chopped

Freshly grated Parmesan cheese

★ TIP ★

You can use a spiralizer, julienne peeler or mandoline to make squash noodles.

CHEESY
QUINOA, BROCCOLI
& SAUSAGE
SKILLET

COOK TIME
30
MIN OR LESS

Not only is quinoa packed with protein, it's very versatile. And it really pulls this delectable dish together.

---

1   Grill sausages on the Johnsonville® Sizzling Sausage Grill™ (or cook using your favorite method). Cool slightly; cut into ½-inch slices and set aside.

2   While sausage is cooking, heat olive oil in a large skillet over medium heat. Add garlic and sauté until fragrant, about 2 minutes.

3   Add quinoa and cook for 2 minutes. Add broth and simmer for 10 minutes.

4   Add broccoli and red pepper, and simmer until quinoa is thoroughly cooked and broccoli is tender.

5   Add sausage and cheese; toss to combine.

INGREDIENTS

- 3   links Johnsonville® Mild or Hot Italian Sausage
- 1   tablespoon olive oil
- 2   cloves garlic, minced
- 1   cup uncooked quinoa
- 1½   cups vegetable broth
- 2   cups broccoli florets
- ½   cup red pepper, diced
- 1   cup shredded cheddar cheese

CHORIZO + QUINOA
ENCHILADA BAKE

Chorizo is an obvious choice for these tasty enchiladas. It's easy to throw all these delicious ingredients into a baking dish and come back 15 minutes later for a hot meal.

1 (19-ounce) package Johnsonville® Chorizo Sausage Links

1 cup quinoa, cooked

2 cans enchilada sauce

1 red bell pepper, diced

1 green bell pepper, diced

2 cups corn kernels

2 cups black beans, drained

1 jalapeño, diced

2 cups shredded Mexican-blend cheese

1 Preheat oven to 375°F.

2 Grill chorizo on the Johnsonville® Sizzling Sausage Grill™ (or cook using your favorite method). Cool slightly; cut into ½-inch slices and set aside.

3 Combine sausage slices, cooked quinoa, enchilada sauce, peppers, corn, black beans, jalapeño and cheese; toss to combine.

4 Bake until bubbly, about 15 minutes.

INGREDIENTS

- 1 (19-ounce) package Johnsonville® Original Brats
- ¼ cup soy sauce
- 1 tablespoon fish sauce
- 1 tablespoon garlic, minced
- 2 tablespoons sugar
- 1 tablespoon peanut oil
- ½ cup yellow onion, chopped
- ⅓ cup chili garlic sauce
- 3 cups fresh stir fry vegetables (carrots, broccoli, peppers and snow peas)
- 5 green onions, chopped
- 2 (8.8-ounce) packages white or brown rice, cooked

ASIAN-INSPIRED
SAUSAGE RICE BOWL

COOK TIME 30 MIN OR LESS

Brats might not be the first thing that come to mind when you think of stir fry, but after one bite of this dish, you'll never think twice again.

1   Grill brats on the Johnsonville® Sizzling Sausage Grill™ (or cook using your favorite method). Cool slightly; cut into ½-inch slices and set aside.

2   While sausage is cooking, combine soy sauce, fish sauce, garlic and sugar in a small bowl. Set aside.

3   Add peanut oil to a large nonstick skillet over medium-high heat. Add onion and sauté until soft, about 4 to 5 minutes. Add soy sauce mixture and stir to incorporate; cook for about 1 minute.

4   Add sausage and mix together until fully incorporated; continue cooking for about 2 minutes.

5   Add stir fry vegetables and green onions, and mix together with the sausage. Cook and stir until vegetables have reached desired doneness.
NOTE: *If you need more liquid, just add some water.*

6   Serve in individual bowls over white or brown rice.

1 (19-ounce) package Johnsonville® Mild or Hot Italian Sausage Links

1 tablespoon olive oil

1 large onion, diced

1 green pepper, diced

1 red pepper, diced

1 (14-ounce) can tomato sauce

½ cup water

½ cup roasted garlic, minced

½ cup pitted Kalamata olives, cut in half lengthwise

3 cups steamed Jasmine rice

ITALIAN SAUSAGE & PEPPER
RICE BOWL

This dish takes all the flavors and ingredients from an Italian sausage sandwich and puts them over a bowl of steamed rice. Easier to eat, if you ask us.

1   Grill Italian sausages on the Johnsonville® Sizzling Sausage Grill™ (or cook using your favorite method). Cool slightly; cut into ½-inch slices and set aside.

2   While sausage is cooking, heat olive oil in a large skillet over medium heat; add onion and peppers, and sauté until tender.

3   When vegetables are mostly cooked through, pour tomato sauce into the middle of the pan and add water.

4   Simmer until everything is thoroughly cooked and the flavors blend.

5   Add sausage, garlic and olives; stir to combine.

6   Serve over rice in individual bowls.

INGREDIENTS

- 1 (19-ounce) package Johnsonville® Mild or Hot Italian Sausage Links
- 2 tablespoons olive oil
- 6 cloves garlic, thinly sliced
- ½ cup onion, diced
- 2 (6-ounce) packages fresh baby spinach
- ⅛ teaspoon crushed red pepper
- Salt and pepper, to taste
- 4 cups steamed brown rice
- ¼ cup freshly grated Parmesan cheese

SPINACH & SAUSAGE
RICE BOWL

Brown rice and spinach make this a healthy meal the whole family will love any day of the week. Makes for great leftovers, too.

———

1 Grill Italian sausages on the Johnsonville® Sizzling Sausage Grill™ (or cook using your favorite method). Cool slightly; cut into ½-inch slices and set aside.

2 While sausage is cooking, heat olive oil in a large skillet over medium heat. Add garlic and onion, and sauté until tender-crisp.

3 Add sausage, spinach and red pepper; sauté until spinach wilts slightly. Season with salt and pepper.

4 Spoon rice into a bowl and top with sausage-and-spinach mixture. Top with a sprinkle of Parmesan cheese.

INGREDIENTS

2 links Johnsonville® Mild Italian Sausage

2 eggplants

2 cups cooked quinoa

1 egg

4 cloves garlic, minced

1 teaspoon salt

½ teaspoon pepper

1 teaspoon minced fresh sage

½ cup Parmesan cheese

1 (24-ounce) jar tomato sauce

SAUSAGE & QUINOA
STUFFED EGGPLANT

Eggplant is such a wonderful vessel for packing flavor together. Like true Italian cooking, simple ingredients create a balanced, healthful, bursting-with-flavor dish.

1   Preheat oven to 350°F.

2   Grill Italian sausage on the Johnsonville® Sizzling Sausage Grill™ (or cook using your favorite method). Cool slightly; dice and set aside.

3   While sausage is cooking, cut each eggplant in half lengthwise and discard seeds.

4   Mix together quinoa, sausage, egg, garlic, salt, pepper, sage and cheese; stir to combine.

5   Fill each eggplant half with quinoa mixture and bake for 45 minutes.

6   Serve with tomato sauce over top.

THESE RECIPES were graciously provided by Christine Ferragamo. Christine is a serious foodie who showcases her culinary chops on her blog Chef on High Heels.

Christine and her husband, Salvatore — close family friends of Ralph and Shelly Stayer — live in Florence, Italy, and are involved in the operations of il Borro winery. Salvatore, the grandson of Italian shoe designer Salvatore Ferragamo (June 5, 1898—August 7, 1960), also is involved in olive oil production and hotels.

COOK TIME **30** MIN OR LESS

PENNE
WITH SAUSAGE & ZUCCHINI

Penne is always a favorite, but we add a bit of heavy cream to make this creamy and indulgent.

1 Grill Italian sausage on the Johnsonville® Sizzling Sausage Grill™ (or cook using your favorite method). Cool slightly; slice and set aside.

2 While sausage is cooking, boil pasta for 8 to 10 minutes. Strain in colander.

3 In a medium saucepan, heat olive oil over medium heat, and sauté onion and zucchini until soft.

4 Add pasta, sausage, parsley, salt, pepper, cheese, chili-pepper flakes (if desired) and heavy cream. Cook for 2 minutes or until pasta reaches desired consistency and cheese is melted.

INGREDIENTS

- 2 links Johnsonville® Mild Italian Sausage
- 1 box (16-ounce) penne, uncooked
- 2 tablespoons olive oil
- 1 cup chopped onion
- 2 small zucchini, cut into cubes
- ¼ cup finely chopped fresh parsley
- 1 teaspoon salt
- ½ teaspoon pepper
- ½ cup shredded Parmesan cheese
- 1 teaspoon chili-pepper flakes (optional)
- ½ cup heavy cream

7

PASTA

- 1 (19-ounce) package Johnsonville® Mild or Hot Italian Sausage Links
- 1 (1-pound) package farfalle (bow-tie) pasta
- 3 tablespoons olive oil
- 1 medium zucchini, thinly sliced
- 15 cherry tomatoes, halved
- 1 medium onion, sliced into thin wedges
- 3 garlic cloves, minced

  Salt and pepper, to taste

BOW-TIE PASTA

COOK TIME **30** MIN OR LESS

Forget heavy sauces—this light and refreshing dish relies on a drizzle of good olive oil and some fresh garlic.

---

1 Grill Italian sausages on the Johnsonville® Sizzling Sausage Grill™ (or cook using your favorite method). Cool slightly; cut into ½-inch slices and set aside.

2 While sausage is cooking, cook pasta according to package directions.

3 Meanwhile, heat olive oil in a large skillet. Add zucchini, tomatoes, onion and garlic. Sauté for 2 to 3 minutes or until tender.

4 Add sausage and heat through.

5 Drain pasta, then add to sausage mixture. Toss to combine. Season with salt and pepper, and serve immediately.

COOK TIME **30** MIN OR LESS

CREAMY
PESTO GNOCCHI
WITH ITALIAN SAUSAGE

Italian sausage pairs so well with this dish, which is as delicate as it is delectably filling.

---

1   Grill Italian sausages on the Johnsonville® Sizzling Sausage Grill™ (or cook using your favorite method). Cool slightly; cut into ¼-inch slices.

2   While sausage is cooking, cook pasta in a large pot or Dutch oven according to package directions. Drain, rinse and return to pot.

3   Meanwhile, in a large skillet, heat olive oil over medium heat, and sauté peppers and peas until crisp-tender. Add to pasta.

4   Add sausage to pasta mixture. Return pot to stove top. Over low heat, stir to combine all ingredients. Add pesto and half-and-half; toss gently to coat all ingredients.

5   Heat through, and sprinkle with cheese to serve.

INGREDIENTS

1   (19-ounce) package Johnsonville® Sweet Italian Sausage Links

1   (16-ounce) package gnocchi pasta

2   tablespoons olive oil

1   medium sweet red bell pepper, diced

8   ounces fresh sugar snap peas (about 2 cups), trimmed

1   cup prepared or homemade pesto

1   cup half-and-half

    Freshly grated Parmesan cheese, for garnish

PAPPARDELLE
WITH ITALIAN SAUSAGE & MUSHROOMS

COOK TIME
30
MIN OR LESS

Pappardelle is one of our favorite pasta types. Since it's such a thick noodle, the flavor of the pasta really shines. So make sure to splurge and get a high-quality brand at your local deli or market.

1   Grill Italian sausages on the Johnsonville® Sizzling Sausage Grill™ (or cook using your favorite method). Cool slightly; small dice or cut into ½-inch slices and set aside.

2   While sausage is cooking, cook pasta according to package directions.

3   Meanwhile, in a large skillet, heat olive oil over medium heat; add mushrooms and sauté until tender.

4   Add garlic and red pepper flakes; season with salt and pepper. Add sliced sausage, cooked pasta, lemon juice and Parmesan cheese, and toss.

5   Garnish with freshly grated Parmesan cheese and parsley, and serve.

Ingredients

1   (19-ounce) package Johnsonville® Mild or Hot Italian Sausage Links

1   package pappardelle pasta

3   tablespoons olive oil

1   pound mushrooms of your choice, cleaned and cut into quarters

1   garlic clove, finely chopped

1   teaspoon dried red pepper flakes, or to taste

Salt and freshly ground black pepper, to taste

Juice of ½ lemon

½   cup freshly grated Parmesan cheese, plus extra for garnish

Chopped fresh parsley, for garnish

INGREDIENTS

- 3 tablespoons olive oil
- 1 sweet onion, diced
- 1 red bell pepper, julienned
- 1 green pepper, julienned
- 4 cloves garlic, minced
- 1 teaspoon dried thyme
- 1 teaspoon dried basil
- 1 medium carrot, finely shredded
- 2 (28-ounce) cans crushed tomatoes
- Salt, to taste
- 1 (19-ounce) package Johnsonville® Mild Italian Sausage Links
- 1 (12-ounce) package pasta of your choice
- Freshly grated Parmesan cheese, for garnish

ITALIAN SAUSAGE & PEPPER
MEDLEY PASTA

This is kind of like an Italian sandwich in a bowl—and much less messy to eat.

———

1 In a large saucepan, heat olive oil and add onion, peppers and garlic. Cook over medium heat until onions are translucent, about 10 minutes.

2 Add thyme, basil and carrot, and cook for 5 more minutes.

3 Add tomatoes and bring to a boil.

4 Lower heat to medium-low and cook for 30 minutes. Season with salt.

5 Meanwhile, grill Italian sausages on the Johnsonville® Sizzling Sausage Grill™ (or cook using your favorite method). Cool slightly; cut into ½-inch slices and add to sauce.

6 Cook pasta according to package directions; drain.

7 Serve sauce over pasta, and top with cheese.

SERVINGS 6 ⏱ **PREP 20 MIN** ⏱ **COOK 15 MIN**

INGREDIENTS

- 1 (19-ounce) package Johnsonville® Mild Italian Sausage Links
- 1 (12-ounce) package rigatoni pasta
- 1 tablespoon olive oil
- 2 cloves garlic, minced
- 1 medium red pepper, thinly sliced
- 1 medium yellow bell pepper, thinly sliced
- 1 medium onion, thinly sliced
- 1 (28-ounce) can diced tomatoes with Italian herbs

  Freshly grated Parmesan cheese, for garnish

  Chopped fresh parsley, for garnish

RIGATONI À LA YOU!

COOK TIME
30
MIN OR LESS

A colorful, zesty meal that satisfies everyone at the table.

———

1 Grill Italian sausages on the Johnsonville® Sizzling Sausage Grill™ (or cook using your favorite method). Cool slightly; cut into ½-inch slices and set aside.

2 While sausage is cooking, cook pasta according to package directions; keep warm.

3 Meanwhile, in a large pan, heat olive oil and add garlic; sauté lightly for 30 seconds.

4 Add peppers and onion and cook until crisp-tender.

5 Combine sausage and tomatoes with peppers, and heat until warm.

6 Serve sauce over pasta and sprinkle with cheese. Top with fresh parsley.

SHELLS
WITH ITALIAN SAUSAGE & RICOTTA STUFFING

Shells and cheese are a staple for any family. We add sausage to leave your stomach extra happy and full.

———

1 Cook pasta according to package directions; drain and rinse with cold water.

2 While pasta is cooking, grill Italian sausages on the Johnsonville® Sizzling Sausage Grill™ (or cook using your favorite method). Cool slightly; small dice or cut into ½-inch slices and set aside.

3 Preheat oven to 350°F.

4 Using a pastry brush, coat the sides and bottom of a 15-by-10-by-2-inch baking dish with olive oil. Pour half of sauce on the bottom of the baking dish and set aside.

5 In a large bowl, beat together eggs, ricotta, 2½ cups of mozzarella, ½ cup of Parmesan and Romano. Add basil, pepper and sausage, and stir to combine.

6 Fill each cooked shell with sausage mixture and nestle in sauce. Once all shells are filled, top them with remaining sauce, 1½ cups of mozzarella and ½ cup of Parmesan.

7 Bake, covered, until bubbly, about 45 minutes.

8 Uncover and continue baking about 5 more minutes. Let stand for 5 minutes; sprinkle with parsley and serve.

INGREDIENTS

- 1 (12.5-ounce) package jumbo shells
- 1 (19-ounce) package Johnsonville® Mild or Sweet Italian Sausage Links
- 1 tablespoon olive oil
- 2 (25-ounce) jars marinara sauce, or 5 to 6 cups of your favorite sauce, divided
- 2 large eggs
- 1 (15-ounce) tub ricotta cheese, whole or part-skim
- 4 cups shredded mozzarella cheese, divided
- 1 cup grated Parmesan cheese, divided
- ½ cup grated Romano cheese
- ¼ cup fresh basil, chopped, or 1 tablespoon, dried
- ½ teaspoon freshly ground black pepper
- 2 tablespoons fresh parsley, chopped, or 1 teaspoon, dried

COOK TIME
30
MIN OR LESS

INGREDIENTS

- 1 (19-ounce) package Johnsonville® Hot Italian Sausage Links
- 1 tablespoon olive oil
- 1 medium sweet bell pepper, diced
- 1 cup mushrooms, sliced
- 1 clove garlic, minced
- ½ cup red wine
- 1 (16-ounce) jar Alfredo sauce
- 1 pound penne pasta, cooked and drained
- ½ cup Parmesan cheese

SPICY SAUSAGE
PASTA ALFREDO

There are dozens of delicious Alfredo variations, but this is one of our favorites. Who wouldn't love the red wine addition?

---

1 Grill Italian sausages on the Johnsonville® Sizzling Sausage Grill™ (or cook using your favorite method). Cool slightly; cut into ½-inch slices and set aside.

2 While sausage is cooking, heat olive oil in a large skillet. Add pepper, mushrooms and garlic; sauté until tender.

3 Add wine and continue to cook until half of the liquid has evaporated.

4 Stir in sausage, sauce, pasta and cheese until blended. Serve immediately.

SPINACH FETTUCCINE
WITH SAUSAGE, PEPPERS & OLIVES

COOK TIME
30
MIN OR LESS

A very sophisticated side of pasta. Simple to make, and wonderful for a dinner party.

---

1   Grill Italian sausages on the Johnsonville® Sizzling Sausage Grill™ (or cook using your favorite method). Cool slightly; small dice or cut into ½-inch slices and set aside.

2   While sausage is cooking, cook pasta according to package directions; drain and set aside.

3   Heat olive oil in a large skillet. Add onion and cook for 2 to 3 minutes.

5   Add garlic and red pepper, and cook for 3 to 4 more minutes.

6   Add tomatoes and cook 4 to 5 minutes or until vegetables are crisp-tender.

7   Stir in sausage, olives and basil.

8   Toss pasta with sausage mixture. Sprinkle with cheese and serve.

INGREDIENTS

1   (19-ounce) package Johnsonville® Mild or Hot Italian Sausage Links

1   (9-ounce) package spinach fettuccine

¼   cup olive oil

1   large onion, sliced

3   large cloves garlic, minced

1   red pepper, sliced

5   large Italian plum tomatoes, chopped

¾   cup Kalamata olives, pitted and halved

½   cup chopped fresh basil

½   cup shredded Parmesan cheese

INGREDIENTS

- 8 ounces tube pasta
- 1 (19-ounce) package Johnsonville® Mild Italian Sausage Links
- 1 (24-ounce) jar marinara sauce
- 2 eggs, beaten
- 1 (15-ounce) carton ricotta cheese
- 2½ cups shredded mozzarella cheese, divided
- ½ cup shredded Parmesan cheese
- ¼ cup chopped fresh basil, for garnish

FAST 'N' EASY
BAKED ZITI

This is a go-to for any family during busy school and work nights.

1 Cook pasta according to package directions; drain and set aside.

2 While pasta is cooking, grill Italian sausages on the Johnsonville® Sizzling Sausage Grill™ (or cook using your favorite method). Cool slightly; cut into ½-inch slices.

3 Preheat oven to 350°F.

4 In a bowl, combine sausage and marinara sauce.

5 In a separate bowl, combine eggs, ricotta cheese, 1½ cups mozzarella cheese and Parmesan cheese; mix well.

6 Add pasta to cheese mixture, and toss to coat.

7 In a greased 13-by-9-by-2-inch baking dish, layer half of pasta mixture and half of meat sauce. Repeat layers.

8 Cover and bake for 30 minutes. Remove and sprinkle with remaining mozzarella cheese. Bake, uncovered, for 5 to 10 more minutes or until cheese is melted.

9 Let stand for 15 minutes before serving. Sprinkle with basil.

8

PIZZA

COOK TIME
30
MIN OR LESS

INGREDIENTS

- 1 package pizza dough mix
- 1 (19-ounce) package Johnsonville® Mild Italian Sausage Links
- 3 tablespoons olive oil, divided
- 1 medium onion, cut into thin strips
- 4 cloves garlic, finely chopped
- 8 ounces mushrooms, sliced thick
- 5 ounces mozzarella cheese, shredded
- 1 teaspoon lemon juice
- 3 ounces shredded Parmesan cheese
- ½ teaspoon red pepper flakes

TUSCAN
SAUSAGE PIZZA

Humble ingredients combine for an indulgent pizza packed with flavor.

1 Position oven rack in center of oven and preheat oven to 400°F.

2 Follow package directions to make pizza dough. Stretch or roll pizza onto a sheet pan or pizza baking plate.

3 Grill Italian sausages on the Johnsonville® Sizzling Sausage Grill™ (or cook using your favorite method). Cool slightly; small dice or cut into ½-inch slices and set aside.

4 While sausage is cooking, heat a 10-inch sauté pan over medium heat. Add 2 tablespoons of olive oil and, in batches, individually cook onion, mushrooms and garlic. Remove each to its own small bowl. Set aside.

5 Brush remaining tablespoon of olive oil on pizza dough. Top with mozzarella, then cover with sausage slices. Cover evenly with garlic, onion and mushrooms.

6 Sprinkle pizza with lemon juice, Parmesan and red pepper flakes. Place on the middle rack of the oven and cook for 20 minutes, or until crust is crisp and cheese is bubbly.

7 Cut into wedges or squares to serve.

PIZZA CUCINA

COOK TIME
30
MIN OR LESS

Gorgonzola cheese, peppers and olives piled on a thin crust—this deliciously unique combination puts a new spin on classic sausage pizza.

———

1 Position oven rack in center of oven and preheat to 425°F.

2 Grill Italian sausages on the Johnsonville® Sizzling Sausage Grill™ (or cook using your favorite method). Cool slightly; small dice or cut into ½-inch slices and set aside.

3 Place pizza crust on a baking sheet. Spread sauce over crust, leaving a ¾-inch border around the edge.

4 Layer with ¾ cup mozzarella, ¾ of the basil, sausage, ½ cup Gorgonzola, olives, remaining mozzarella, bell pepper and remaining Gorgonzola.

5 Bake pizza for 13 minutes until crust is crisp and topping is heated through.

6 Remove from oven, sprinkle with remaining basil, cut and enjoy!

INGREDIENTS

- 1 (19-ounce) package Johnsonville® Hot Italian Sausage Links
- 1 thin premade pizza crust
- 1 cup marinara sauce
- 1¼ cups shredded mozzarella cheese, divided
- ½ cup fresh basil leaves, thinly sliced, divided
- 1 cup crumbled Gorgonzola cheese, divided
- ¼ cup Kalamata olives or other brine-cured black olives, pitted and halved
- 4 sliced rings of green bell pepper, quartered

SERVINGS **4-6** ⏱ PREP **15** MIN ⏱ COOK **20** MIN

SAUSAGE FLORENTINE

FLATBREAD

This dish perfectly captures the essence of the signature Florentine flavor.

- 1 (19-ounce) package Johnsonville® Hot Italian Sausage Links
- 2 tablespoons olive oil
- 1 cup fresh mushrooms, sliced
- 2 cloves garlic, minced
- 1 cup pizza sauce
- ½ teaspoon dried oregano
- ½ teaspoon dried basil
- 1 cup spinach (frozen chopped, thawed and well drained)

  Sea salt and pepper, to taste
- 1 package premade flatbread
- 1 cup shredded mozzarella cheese
- ¼ cup fresh basil, sliced (optional)

1 Position oven rack in center of oven and preheat to 400°F.

2 Grill Italian sausages on the Johnsonville® Sizzling Sausage Grill™ (or cook using your favorite method). Cool slightly; small dice or cut into ½-inch slices and set aside.

3 While sausage is cooking, heat olive oil in a large skillet, and sauté mushrooms and garlic.

4 Add sausage, pizza sauce, oregano, basil and spinach; season with salt and pepper. Cook, stirring frequently, until hot.

5 Spread sausage mixture evenly over flatbread crust. Sprinkle with mozzarella.

6 Bake for 8 to 10 minutes or until cheese is bubbly. Remove from oven and sprinkle with fresh basil if desired. Cut and serve.

- 2 (13.8-ounce) tubes refrigerated pizza dough
- 1 (19-ounce) package Johnsonville® Mild Italian Sausage Links
- 1 cup ricotta cheese
- 2 cups shredded mozzarella cheese
- ⅔ cup crumbled Gorgonzola cheese
- ½ cup shredded Parmesan cheese
- 2 teaspoons chopped fresh herbs (optional)

QUATTRO FORMAGGI
PIZZA

Cheese lovers, unite! Ricotta, mozzarella, Gorgonzola and Parmesan: This pizza is a celebration of the heavy-hitters in Italian flavor.

1 Preheat oven to 400°F. Prebake pizza crusts according to package directions. Allow to cool slightly.

2 Meanwhile, grill Italian sausages on the Johnsonville® Sizzling Sausage Grill™ (or cook using your favorite method). Cool slightly; small dice or cut into ½-inch slices and set aside.

3 Spread ½ cup ricotta over each crust. Top with mozzarella, Gorgonzola, sausage and Parmesan.

4 Bake for 10 to 12 minutes, or until crust is golden brown and cheese is bubbly.

5 Remove from oven and sprinkle with fresh herbs, if desired.

CAULIFLOWER
PIZZA CRUST

Looking for a lighter pizza crust? This dish uses low-carb cauliflower instead of traditional dough.

---

1 Preheat oven to 450°F. Line a baking sheet with parchment paper.

2 Cut cauliflower into florets, then pulse in a food processor or grate by hand on a box grater. Steam in a steamer basket or in the microwave, until tender. Drain well; blot with paper towel to remove any excess water.

3 In a bowl, combine basil, oregano, garlic powder, salt and pepper, and egg. Mix well. Transfer cauliflower mixture to parchment-lined baking sheet; press and shape into a pizza crust. Bake for 15 minutes.

4 Add desired toppings and bake for an additional 10 minutes, or until crust is golden brown and cheese is bubbly.

INGREDIENTS

1 head cauliflower, stalk removed

½ teaspoon dried basil

½ teaspoon dried oregano

½ teaspoon garlic powder

Salt and pepper, to taste

1 egg, beaten

ACKNOWLEDGMENTS

WE'D LIKE TO THANK the following team members for their instrumental roles in the development of the Johnsonville® Sizzling Sausage Grill™.

Kevin Addesso

Anne Addesso

Tom Schneider

Yan Zhao

Melissa Reichwald

Art Kleine

Tony Rammer

Rachelle Kolste

Steve Neumeyer

Jim Varney

Hong Ji

INDEX

Page numbers in italics indicate photos.

———————

SHELLY STAYER

Shelly Stayer is the co-owner of Johnsonville® Sausage, the inventor of the Sizzling Sausage Grill™ and an all-around "mom-preneur"—she's been awarded Entrepreneur of the Year in both Wisconsin and Florida. She and her husband, Ralph C. Stayer, own Johnsonville® Sausage, the largest seller of sausage in the United States and 40 countries. Ralph and Shelly live in Naples, Florida, where her involvement in community relations has helped countless children and families in-need, and earned her several awards in both Florida and her home-state of Wisconsin. *The Sizzling Sausage Cookbook* is Shelly's third book, the others being *Big Taste of Sausage Cookbook* and *The Weight of a Father's Shadow*. Together, Ralph and Shelly have seven children, several of whom are involved in the family business.